Spotlight on Strategic Priorities for School Improvement

Edited by Caroline T. Chauncey

No. 6 in the *Harvard Education Letter* Spotlight Series

HARVARD EDUCATION PRESS
CAMBRIDGE, MASSACHUSETTS

Library of Congress Control Number 2009942751

Paperback ISBN 978-1-934742-61-7
Library Edition ISBN 978-1-934742-62-4

Published by Harvard Education Press, an imprint of the Harvard Education Publishing Group

Harvard Education Press
8 Story Street
Cambridge, MA 02138

Cover Design: Sarah Henderson

The typefaces used in this book are Humanist 777 for text and Kuenstler 480 for display.

Contents

Foreword

The Obama Administration's Race to the Top (RTTT) competition has sparked more energy and enthusiasm among state leaders than any federal education initiative in recent memory. Given the intense controversy and polarization that has surrounded the implementation of the No Child Left Behind Act (NCLB) over the last several years, what accounts for this turnaround? One major difference, of course, is that participation in RTTT is voluntary, while NCLB is mandatory, but the dire financial condition of virtually all states in 2010 has meant that all but a handful are expected to file RTTT applications. More to the point, while RTTT may be voluntary, it is significantly more prescriptive than NCLB, asking states to commit to requirements that important stakeholders, especially teacher organizations, have traditionally resisted.

In my view, the surprisingly positive response to RTTT derives from the fact that the four major issues states must address in their applications reflect an accurate understanding of the next level of work states and districts must undertake if the initial promise of standards-based reform is to be realized. After twenty years of experience there is very little pushback to the core ideas of the standards movement: we need to define clear expectations for what all students need to know and be able to do in each core subject at key grade levels, especially the end of high school; measure progress regularly against those expectations; align resources accordingly, paying special attention to the students at greatest risk of not meeting standards; and hold schools accountable for results. There is widespread recognition, however, that it is one thing to enunciate these principles and quite another to be able to implement them in ways that will genuinely enable all students to leave high school college-and/or career-ready. While there are no magic bullets for educational improvement, the Obama administration is betting that the states that adopt more rigorous standards and richer assessments, develop more powerful data systems, invest in the development of great teachers and leaders, and aggressively focus on turning around their lowest-performing schools will show the most progress in improving student performance in the next decade.

The thoughtful essays in this volume can provide useful guidance to policymakers and practitioners as they move to address these four areas for improvement. Most of these essays, which originally appeared in the *Harvard Education Letter*, were written well before the RTTT competition was announced; nonetheless, they speak to the major reform elements that state and district plans are asked to address, and offer practical advice on key implementation challenges.

STANDARDS AND ASSESSMENTS

NCLB has had two major consequences—one intended; the other, not. The intended consequence has been to redefine our concept of a successful school from one that on average performs well to one in which all groups of students are making reasonable annual progress. NCLB's insistence that schools and districts report student achievement results disaggregated by race, economic status, language status, and special needs has been almost entirely salutary and is likely to remain an essential feature of federal education policy.

NCLB's unintended consequence, however, has been to build unprecedented support among education leaders for common academic standards that all states can adopt. NCLB underscored the absurdity of trying to superimpose a federal accountability system on fifty states after each has developed its own standards, adopted its own assessment system, and determined its own definition of academic proficiency. Unlike previous attempts to develop national standards at the federal level, the current effort is being led by two organizations that represent the states, the National Governors Association and the Council of Chief State School Officers, and the goal is to develop standards that are fewer in number, written in language that is clear to laypeople as well as teachers, and benchmarked against higher-performing nations as well as the expectations of colleges and employers.

One huge advantage of buying into common standards is that the states can then pool resources to develop much higher quality assessments, and the Obama administration has set aside $350 million from the RTTT program to support assessment development among consortia of states. This should enable states and districts to shift attention and resources away from end-of-year assessments and invest more heavily in the kinds of formative assessments that can give teachers the timely, ongoing feedback they need in order to adjust their instructional practice to meet their students' needs. There is a huge demand among teachers for what one contributor to this volume calls "(in)formative assessments" and others have called "assessments *for* learning"; I anticipate that most RTTT winners will set aside funds to invest in the development of more instructionally useful assessments.

USING DATA TO IMPROVE INSTRUCTION

In a relatively short period schools have gone from being data poor to drowning in data. A big challenge throughout the sector is to help principals and teachers become savvy, sophisticated users of data—what the authors of two essays in this volume call "data wise." This means enabling teams of teachers at the building level to learn to analyze assessment and other student data together and then make the necessary changes in organizational processes and classroom practices to improve student outcomes.

GREAT TEACHERS AND LEADERS

If there is a single major lesson policymakers have learned from education research over the past decade, it is that teachers really matter, especially for high-need children. Three great teachers in a row for low-income and minority kids in the early grades can virtually wipe out the achievement gap. Three poor teachers in a row can put similar kids so far behind their peers that their chances of ever catching up are very small. Consequently, states and districts across the country are scrambling to recruit and develop high-quality teachers, and human capital organizations like Teach for America and The New Teacher Project that supply new talent are in great demand.

But getting highly talented people to enter the teaching profession is one thing; keeping them in the profession is quite another. As a consequence, states and districts are now paying more attention to the need for much stronger mentoring and support programs for teachers in their early years, as well as the need to create new roles that enable teachers to exercise more leadership without having to leave the classroom. There is also growing pressure, as evidenced in the RTTT application criteria, for districts to incorporate evidence of student learning into the teacher evaluation process, and to redesign compensation systems not only to reward teachers who take on additional leadership responsibilities but also to recognize teachers whose students make more academic progress than expected.

TURNING AROUND STRUGGLING SCHOOLS

Perhaps the single biggest political challenge states and districts face is that of turning around their lowest-performing schools. Because we now know just how important great teachers are for our neediest students, the question is how to motivate a much larger proportion of our very best teachers to work in our most challenging schools. Thanks to the work of Karin Chenoweth and other talented journalists and researchers, we now know quite a bit about the characteristics of high-poverty/high-achieving schools. One thing we know is that the principal is key. The best way to convince really good teachers to go into tough schools is to appoint a great principal and give that principal the tools and flexibility he or she needs to build a great teaching team.

From the work of Richard Elmore and others, we also know that school improvement is not a linear process, and that two schools whose test results are similar may be at very different places on the improvement path. Some low-performing schools may have such a weak or toxic culture that emptying the building of the current adult population and starting over with new management may be the only viable strategy, while others may need only more time and some focused technical assistance to get unstuck and begin moving forward. The lesson here is that an accountability system that relies solely on quantitative measures and does not incorporate some method for injecting informed human judgment into the evaluation process will more often than not miss the mark.

While these four areas hardly constitute an exhaustive reform agenda, research and experience suggest that states and districts that invest in developing and implementing high-quality formative assessments, provide ongoing support to their educators in the use of data, create pathways to attract and retain talented teachers and principals, and provide incentives and supports for strong leaders and teachers to work in their most challenging schools are likely to see improved outcomes for students. This volume is designed to provide practical guidance for educators choosing to pursue this ambitious agenda.

Robert B. Schwartz
Academic Dean and William Henry Bloomberg Professor,
Harvard Graduate School of Education

Introduction

Caroline T. Chauncey

The advent of the American Recovery and Reinvestment Act and the announcement of the Obama administration's $4 billion Race to the Top initiative marked a radical shift in the federal government's approach to education reform, one whose impact is likely to be felt for years to come. As Robert B. Schwartz points out in the Foreword to this volume, the four criteria for winning funding under the Race to the Top program provide a framework for "the next level of work" in standards-based reform. These four pillars of strategic reform—standards and assessment, using data to improve instruction, teacher quality and effectiveness, and a commitment to turning around failing schools—along with district-based improvement, also constitute the organizing framework for this book.

Strategic Priorities for School Improvement, the sixth volume in the *Harvard Education Letter* Spotlight series, brings together 18 recent articles that carefully examine key elements of success in each of these core areas of education reform. Bringing together the voices of leading education journalists, practitioners, and scholars, the articles collected here offer a blend of insight, evidence, and practical information aimed at helping school and district leaders navigate the demands of this challenging new era.

Part I opens with a thoughtful and provocative analysis by noted assessment expert W. James Popham. Looking back over his long career, he identifies six "unlearned lessons"—key mistakes that continue to inhibit schools' success. Prominent among these problems are the proliferation of curricular targets (too many standards) and the ineffective use of assessment, issues that are highly relevant to the recent move toward common academic standards and student assessments.

Two chapters by veteran education journalist Robert Rothman flesh out the discussion of assessment. In chapter 2, Rothman offers a pragmatic guide to the effective use of formative assessment, a powerful classroom tool for improving teaching and learning. In chapter 3, he addresses the technical challenges involved in value-added assessment, a hotly debated technique that offers the potential to hold both schools and teachers accountable for growth in student performance. The chapter takes a close look at the promises and limitations of this approach, particularly when applied in the context of existing accountability systems.

The discussion of assessment in the opening section of the book paves the way for part II, "Using Data to Improve Instruction." Chapters 4 and 5 introduce and describe the Data Wise improvement process. This widely successful approach, pioneered as a joint venture between the Harvard Graduate School of Education and the Boston Public Schools, brings teachers together to examine and evaluate student data as they strive to find more effective ways to teach. In addition to providing an overview of the process, the authors take the reader into schools that are implementing Data Wise to learn from their experiences. Finally, in chapter 6, Harvard Graduate School of Education faculty member Lee Teitel describes the process of instructional rounds—an innovative approach to classroom observation based on medical rounds. Designed to help school leaders develop their skills in observing and talking about instruction, this process is critical to creating a shared vision of effective teaching.

Effective instruction is the core issue taken up in part III, "Developing Great Teachers and Leaders." In chapter 7, Robert Rothman takes a detailed look at hiring practices that enable schools to recruit and retain highly qualified teachers. Beyond hiring, however, school and district leaders need to provide support and guidance to help new teachers develop their skills, and to evaluate experienced teachers and to direct their professional growth. In chapter 8, Ellen Moir and her colleagues at the New Teacher Center lay out the principles of a high-quality, instructionally intensive mentoring program for new teachers. In chapter 9, journalist Andreae Downs takes a close look at the Montgomery County (Md.) Public Schools' nationally recognized standards-based system for teacher evaluation and professional development. The last chapter in this section, by Robert Rothman, draws on a series of studies about effective principal preparation to focus on the role of mentorship in preparing qualified school leaders.

"Turning Around Struggling Schools" is the theme of part IV. In chapters 11 and 12, journalists Nancy Walser and Chris Rand, respectively, interview author Karin Chenoweth about her research on "It's Being Done" schools—high-achieving schools with high-poverty, high-minority populations. In the first interview, Chenoweth describes her research identifying schools like these across the country; the second interview, focusing on her subsequent research, digs deep into the factors that account for some of these schools' success.

In chapter 13, Harvard Graduate School of Education faculty members Richard F. Elmore and Elizabeth A. City step back to examine the big picture of school improvement. Contrary to the No Child Left Behind Act's expectation of a straight path toward adequate yearly progress—or, more recently, the pressure to achieve an instant turnaround—the authors describe instead a "hard, bumpy" process that is iterative, developmental, and requires sustained, timely, and appropriate external support. City follows up in chapter 14 with a close look inside schools at the beginning of this process, identifying the kinds of resources such schools are able to draw on—such as hope and trust, as well as people, time, and money—and how best to invest them. Despite their popularity, she argues, investments like coaching may not pay off as effectively as smaller activities that build a shared vision of and commitment to change.

In chapter 15, principal and author D. Brent Stephens takes up Elmore and City's depiction of the developmental nature of school improvement. Given the persistent failure of external intervention, he argues for a new approach that assesses struggling schools' responses to four "foundational dilemmas." These include the *attribution of cause* (where does responsibility for poor student performance lie?); the *control of instruction* (is it centralized or distributed?); the *location of the response to intervention* (out-of-class initiatives versus efforts to improve classroom instruction); and the *definition of the challenge* (is it perceived as a matter of compliance or one of professional learning?).

The final chapter in this section examines the "unorthodox relationship" between charter schools and unions, penned by veteran education journalist Alexander Russo. Although policymakers at the highest levels have looked to a partnership between charters and unions as a potentially groundbreaking approach to school improvement, Russo also points to the many tensions and questions inherent in this approach.

Part V closes the book with two provocative chapters that examine the role of the district in supporting school reform. In chapter 17, authors Rachel E. Curtis and Elizabeth A.

City emphasize the importance of strategy as the backbone of school improvement efforts, focusing particularly on the difference between strategy—"a few high-leverage ways to improve instruction and student learning"—and strategic planning, the accumulation of unrelated initiatives that bog down improvement efforts in so many districts. Chapter 18 draws on the work of the Public Education Leadership Project, a joint initiative of the Harvard Business School and the Harvard Graduate School of Education, to present a framework for creating coherence in district administration, so that a district's improvement strategy is supported at every level and by every stakeholder and constituent.

Taken together, these articles are intended to provide a useful guide for school leaders, education advocates, and policymakers as they seek to navigate the next generation of education reform in the United States.

I would like to thank my colleagues at Harvard Education Press for their ongoing support and in particular to acknowledge with appreciation the assistance of Katrina Swartz in preparing the manuscript.

PART I

Standards and Assessment

CHAPTER 1

Unlearned Lessons

Six stumbling blocks to our schools' success

W. James Popham

I f there's any truth in the saying, "Those who don't learn from their mistakes are destined to repeat them," why is it that today's educators seem almost compelled to replicate their predecessors' blunders?

Having been a public school educator for well over a half-century, I am fed up with seeing today's educators making precisely the same sorts of mistakes I've seen their predecessors make, again and again, in earlier years.

In the following analysis, I will identify a half-dozen mistakes we've made in our schools. Some are mistakes I made myself long ago, as a high school teacher in Oregon or as a teacher educator at state colleges in Kansas and California and at UCLA. Others are mistakes I've observed up close and personal in the course of several decades of work in the field of assessment. Some are errors of commission, while others are errors of omission. All of them are mistakes that have a negative impact on a large number of classrooms. All of them diminish the quality of schooling we provide to our students.

MISTAKE #1: TOO MANY CURRICULAR TARGETS

Educational policymakers have laid out an unreasonably large number of curricular aims for teachers to teach—too many to be taught and too many to be tested. These target aims—usually referred to as content standards, objectives, benchmarks, expectancies, or some synonymous descriptors—tend to resemble a curricular "wish list" rather than a realistic set of attainable educational outcomes. In some states, for example, elementary teachers at each grade level are supposed to teach their students to master 300 or more curricular aims by the end of a given year. Any of the 300 aims may appear on the state's annual accountability assessments.

This problem has plagued us since the 1960s, when the growth of the "behavioral objectives" movement—an effort to identify what learners would be able to do as a result of instruction—resulted in the proliferation of highly detailed objectives (the equivalent of today's curricular aims). While the movement itself was well intended, it ultimately failed because of this problem.

Because teachers are patently unable to get their students to master so many different aims at any defensible level of depth, what happens in many classrooms is a desperate effort in which teachers try to touch on *all* the skills and knowledge their students might encounter in the upcoming accountability tests. But content that has only been touched on is unlikely to make a real difference to students. Superficiality rather than meaningful instruction is fostered.

Moreover, because accountability tests can't possibly include enough items to measure accurately every curricular aim, the people who build those tests are required to *sample* from the skills and knowledge that are eligible to be tested. As a result, many teachers try to guess which curricular aims will actually be on the test. If they guess wrong, the tests wind up measuring content the teachers didn't teach and failing to measure content that they did. Thus the state's annual accountability tests provide a misleading picture of educators' instructional success.

To fix this problem, state educational leaders must reframe their state's curricular aims at a more appropriate level of breadth—that is, at a larger "grain size." Second, they must prioritize the resultant curricular aims so that only the most important can be designated as potentially assessable each year. These broad aims can encompass subsets of lesser skills and knowledge, but must be stated with sufficient clarity so teachers can properly target their instructional activities. Moreover, with fewer curricular aims to assess, the state's test developers can include enough items to measure each one accurately.

MISTAKE #2: THE UNDERUTILIZATION OF CLASSROOM ASSESSMENT

For more than a decade we have had access to empirical research showing conclusively that when teachers employ formative assessment in their classrooms, whopping improvements in students' learning will take place. Yet too many teachers continue to employ classroom assessments exclusively to grade students or to motivate those students to study harder.

Formative assessment is a planned process in which assessment-elicited evidence of students' status is used by teachers to adjust their ongoing instructional procedures or by students to adjust their current learning tactics. Although two seminal articles on formative assessment were published as far back as 1998—one in a prestigious scholarly journal, the other in the widely read *Phi Delta Kappan*, both authored by British researchers Paul Black and Dylan Wiliam—these insights have yet to be applied in classrooms on a large scale.

To the extent that our teachers are not routinely employing classroom formative assessment as part of their regular instructional activities, students are not being as well educated as they could be.

We need to get the word out to the nation's teachers that formative assessment is capable of triggering big boosts in students' achievement—the educational equivalent of a cure for the common cold. For instance, in 2006, the Council of Chief State School Officers (CCSSO) established a standing advisory committee to investigate ways to promote the use of formative assessment. At the same time, CCSSO created a collaborative of about 20 states committed to implementing formative assessment. By 2008, the CCSSO National Conference on Student Assessment was giving substantial attention to formative assessment, in addition to its traditional focus on large-scale assessment. The CCSSO story could obviously be replicated in other associations—associations of teachers and educational administrators, school boards, or other education advocacy groups.

We must also create a variety of mechanisms, for instance, diverse professional development programs and the provision of supportive assessment materials, to help more teachers apply this potent process in their classrooms.

MISTAKE #3: A PREOCCUPATION WITH INSTRUCTIONAL PROCESS

Many teachers focus almost obsessively on the instructional procedures they use, rather than on the impact those procedures have on students. This overriding attention to "what teachers do in class" instead of "whether students learn" seems to have plagued teachers from time immemorial. In practice, it means that teachers spend too little time evaluating the quality of their instructional activities. If instructional activities have not been evaluated, they may be less effective than teachers believe them to be. As a result, many teachers persist in employing instructional activities that are of limited benefit to students.

Teachers who have a clear grasp of the relationship between educational ends and means are more likely to understand the importance of routinely verifying the quality of their instructional procedures (means) according to the impact those procedures have on students (ends). The nature of this means-ends relationship—and the need to evaluate means according to the ends they produce—must be emphasized in the preservice preparation of teachers and administrators. In addition, the nation's leading professional organizations should collaborate to urge educators to pay greater attention to the outcomes of instruction rather than the nature of instructional procedures *per se*.

MISTAKE #4: THE ABSENCE OF AFFECTIVE ASSESSMENT

At this moment in our schools, there is a dearth of assessment instruments suitable for measuring students' affect—that is, students' attitudes, interests, and values. Although most educators, if pushed, will agree that the promotion of appropriate affective outcomes is as important as—and in some instances even more important than—the promotion of students' cognitive achievements, almost no systematic attention is given in our nation's classrooms to the promotion of appropriate affect among students.

This problem dates back at least to the 1950s and 1960s. When Benjamin Bloom and his colleagues published the influential *Taxonomy of Educational Objectives* in 1956, they separated educational objectives into three major categories: cognitive, affective, and psychomotor. The book's focus, however, was almost completely on cognitive objectives. A subsequent volume by David Krathwohl and two coauthors, published in 1964, laid out a hierarchical taxonomy of affective objectives. But the book never enjoyed the success of its cognitive cousin.

Because of this overemphasis on cognition, the affective consequences of instruction are unpredictable and sometimes harmful. For instance, a child who dislikes reading or is intimidated by mathematics develops attitudes in school that are almost certain to have a negative impact on his or her life.

A prominent reason that schools pay little attention to students' affect is the absence of assessment instruments suitable for measuring students' attitudes, interests, and values. At a fairly modest cost, however, governmental and/or nongovernmental agencies could provide teachers with a wide range of survey instruments to be completed anonymously by students, so that teachers can adjust their instructional activities accordingly. Teachers may also benefit from professional development regarding ways to promote appropriate student affect.

MISTAKE #5: INSTRUCTIONALLY INSENSITIVE ACCOUNTABILITY TESTS

Almost all the accountability tests being used to evaluate our nation's schools are incapable of doing so. From the earliest beginnings of the educational accountability movement in America—a movement nearly a half-century old—we've been using the wrong measurement tools to judge the quality of America's schools. Nearly every state-level accountability test tends to measure the composition of a school's student body—what students bring to school in terms of socioeconomic status or inherited academic aptitude—rather than the success with which those students have been taught. As a result, enormous numbers of U.S. schools are currently being inaccurately evaluated. Effective schools are thought to be failing; so-so schools are seen as successful.

These inaccurate evaluations of school quality have both an immediate and long-term harmful impact on our students.

For instance, teachers who are doing a good instructional job, but whose students' test results (inaccurately) indicate otherwise, may abandon effective instructional techniques and adopt less effective ones. Teachers who are doing an inept instructional job, but whose students' test results (inaccurately) indicate otherwise, are apt to continue using unsound teaching procedures. In both of these scenarios, students end up as the losers.

What we must do—immediately—is replace today's instructionally insensitive accountability tests with those that can, with accuracy, sort out schools where students are being well taught from schools where students are not. Evaluating tests for instructional sensitivity could follow the same basic strategy as that used to evaluate items for racial, gender, or class bias—a combination of expert judgment and empirical evidence. An overhaul on this scale will be an expensive undertaking, but the cost and effort are justified by the educational damage caused by our current reliance on instructionally insensitive tests.

MISTAKE #6: ABYSMAL ASSESSMENT LITERACY

At a time when test-based accountability dramatically influences what goes on in our schools, far too few educators understand the fundamentals of educational measurement. Increasingly, however, educational decisions for the nation's youth depend directly on the role of educational tests. Assessment-dependent educational decisions call for assessment-knowledgeable educators. Yet teacher education has not changed to accommodate this demand. Preservice and professional development initiatives need to address two key areas: classroom assessment and accountability assessment. It is patently absurd for teachers and administrators not to understand the instruments by which their professional competence is determined, and on which critical educational decisions are based.

MOXIE, NOT MONEY

Fortunately, almost all of these mistakes can be solved with moxie—not money.

"Moxie"—the slang synonym for courage or boldness—traces its roots to America's first mass-market soft drink. Distributed in Lowell, Mass., during the mid-1920s, Moxie was a fizzed-up version of an 1884 patent-medicine tonic said to cure "brain and nervous exhaustion, loss of manhood, softening of the brain, and mental imbecility." It is small wonder, then, that the name of this popular New England soda soon became a descriptor for someone with plenty of nerve.

Given the current status of the U.S. economy, most improvement strategies we adopt will need to be based on educators' moxie rather taxpayers' largesse. Those involved must be committed to the belief that the problem under consideration warrants attention. I personally believe that each of the six deficits identified here could, if fixed, make a dramatic difference in the way we educate our students. What's needed is a clear commitment to remedying them—and sufficient moxie to make that remedy work.

This chapter is adapted from Unlearned Lessons: Six Stumbling Blocks to Our Schools' Success, *by W. James Popham (Harvard Education Press, 2009), and originally appeared in the March/April 2009 issue of the* Harvard Education Letter.

CHAPTER 2

(In)formative Assessments

New tests and activities can help teachers guide student learning

Robert Rothman

Although many teachers in the age of accountability complain that students take too many tests, teachers at the John D. Philbrick Elementary School in Boston eagerly signed on in 2005 to give students six more tests a year. The tests, known as Formative Assessments of Student Thinking in Reading, or FAST-R, are short multiple-choice quizzes that probe key reading skills. The tests are designed so that teachers can make adjustments to their instruction based on students' answers.

With FAST-R "we get concrete, helpful information on students very quickly," says Steve Zrike, Philbrick's principal.

Now used in 46 schools in Boston, FAST-R is part of a rapidly growing nationwide effort to implement so-called formative assessments—tests that can inform instruction through timely feedback. (By contrast, end-of-term tests and standards-based accountability tests are called summative assessments because they provide a summary of what students have learned.) Interest in formative assessment is fueled by the growing pressure to raise student achievement. Because the state tests on which schools are judged under the No Child Left Behind Act (NCLB) are typically administered at the end of the academic year, educators like Zrike are eager for information that can help them predict whether students are on track toward meeting proficiency goals and then intervene appropriately.

A strong body of evidence indicates that formative assessment, done properly, can generate dramatic improvements in teaching and learning. But some experts warn that many of the instruments marketed as formative assessments are in effect summative tests in disguise. At best such tests provide little useful information to classroom teachers; at worst they can narrow the curriculum and exacerbate the negative effects of teaching to the test, says Lorrie A. Shepard, dean of the School of Education at the University of Colorado at Boulder.

"If all the test produces is a predictive score, or tells you which students to be anxious about, it's a waste of money," she says. True formative assessments, she says, tell teachers "what it is the students aren't understanding."

TASTING THE SOUP

With the proliferation of so many instruments, it's not surprising that many educators find the distinction between formative and summative assessment confusing (see "Three Types of Assessment"). Paul Black, coauthor of a landmark 1998 study on the topic, once described the difference by saying that formative assessment is when the chef tastes the soup; summative assessment is when the customer tastes the soup. As his remark implies, the effectiveness of the process depends not only on the data sampled, but the timeliness of the feedback and how the "chefs"—not only teachers but the students themselves—use it.

In the 1998 study, Black and Dylan Wiliam, both of Kings College, London, examined some 250 studies from around the

THREE TYPES OF ASSESSMENT

	Summative	Benchmark	Formative
Key Question	*Do* you understand? (yes or no)	Is the class on track for proficiency?	*What* do you understand?
When Asked	End of unit/term/year	6–10 times per year	Ongoing
Timing of Results	After instruction ends	Slight delay	Immediate

world and found that the use of formative assessment techniques produced significant accelerations in learning. Students in classes using this approach gained a year's worth of learning in six or seven months. The method appeared particularly effective for low-performing pupils. As a result, formative assessment was found to narrow achievement gaps while it raised achievement overall.

"We know of no other way of raising [achievement] standards," the authors conclude, "for which such a strong prima facie case can be made on the basis of evidence of such large learning gains."

While skilled teachers may be adept at checking for comprehension, identifying misunderstandings, and adjusting instruction accordingly, the authors cited ample research showing the pervasiveness of ineffective or counterproductive assessment techniques in the classroom. "If pilots navigated the way [most] teachers teach," says Wiliam, now deputy director of the Institute of Education in London and former senior research director for the Educational Testing Service (ETS), "they would leave London, head west, and at the end of eight hours, ask, 'Is this New York?'"

Even teachers who check for students' understanding at the end of every lesson seldom get enough information to guide instruction, he adds. "They make up a question at the spur of the moment, ask the whole class, six kids raise their hands, and one answers," Wiliam says. "That's what I did as a teacher. But how dumb is that?"

"Teachers need better data to make instructional decisions," he adds.

THE USES OF BENCHMARK TESTING

Wiliam claims his research has been misinterpreted to suggest that *any* periodic assessment is an effective intervention. Jumping on the formative assessment bandwagon, test publishers have begun selling benchmark or early warning assessments linked to their end-of-year tests that indicate whether students are on track to pass. According to Tim Wiley, a senior analyst at Eduventures, LLC, these assessments represent the fastest-growing segment of the testing industry. Total spending on such instruments is approximately $150 million.

Stuart Kahl, president and CEO of Measured Progress, a testing firm based in Dover, N.H., cautions that benchmark tests are designed to obtain information about groups rather than individuals and should not be confused with formative assessment. The tests usually include only a handful of items on each topic in order to survey knowledge across an entire unit. But while one or two items can provide information on the skills of an entire class or a school, they do not yield enough information about an individual student's understanding to guide instructional decisions. For instance, if three quarters of the class miss both questions on multiplication, the teacher knows she needs to revisit this topic. But are these computational errors or conceptual problems? This kind of test is not likely to reveal the answer for any particular student.

Measured Progress produces a series of benchmark tests known as Progress Toward Standards. Kahl notes that these kinds of tests can be useful for interim program evaluation and for identifying patterns of performance. For example, if girls score better than boys across the board, that may spur schools to examine curriculum and instructional practices. But Kahl agrees with the University of Colorado's Shepard that the interim tests do not provide the type of information about individual student progress that appropriate formative assessments provide.

"Formative assessment is a range of activities at the classroom level [that] teachers use day in and day out to see if kids are getting it while they're teaching it," he says.

FORMATIVE ASSESSMENT TECHNIQUES

Districts and schools using formative assessments employ a variety of techniques. For instance, commercial companies are developing a variety of new assessment tools, ranging from handheld electronic "clickers" that allow students to register their responses to teachers' questions to instructional software programs that incorporate checks on student understanding. This helps teachers gauge the progress of the entire class, not just the students who raise their hands. Some six million students are using such programs at a cost of about $120 million, according to Eduventures' Wiley.

Some curriculum programs also include formative assessment techniques to help teachers gauge student understanding while they are teaching, notes Shepard. For example, a mathematics program might ask students to multiply 3 by 4 in three different ways: by making sets of three, by calculating the area of a floor, and by counting by fours. A right answer on any of these indicates that a student grasps the concept of multiplication. Otherwise, Shepard says, "you don't know if the student doesn't understand the concept or multiplication facts."

At ETS, Wiliam developed a series of workshops called Keeping Learning on Track to help teachers develop formative assessment strategies and monitor their own progress.

These workshops have been conducted in 28 districts, including Cleveland. The workshops revolve around five key strategies: sharing expectations for learning, effective questioning, providing meaningful feedback, student self-assessment, and peer assessment among students. In each district, teachers come together every month to discuss how they implemented the strategies and the results they produced.

Donna Snodgrass, executive director for standards, curriculum, and classroom assessment for the Cleveland public school system, says the effort is essential because state tests provide too little information, and too late, to help teachers in the classroom. By the time the results come back, she notes, "kids are long gone, in another class."

"This gives them an idea of where kids are and what they can do about it," she says.

And it appears to be working. After two years, students' mathematics scores in the 10 participating Cleveland schools—among the lowest-performing in the city—rose four times faster than those in comparable schools. And while the program is aimed particularly at mathematics instruction, the program has also had an effect on reading achievement: reading scores in the 10 schools increased four to five percentage points over two years. Snodgrass says these kinds of results have encouraged teachers to keep trying new strategies. The district is also planning to expand the program to additional schools.

INSIGHT INTO STUDENT MISTAKES

Other districts, like Boston, use more formal assessment instruments. FAST-R, which was developed by the Boston Plan for Excellence, uses 10 multiple-choice questions to probe student comprehension of a particular reading passage. The test can be used as a benchmark assessment, since it is aligned to state end-of-year tests, but it is also designed to help improve reading instruction, says Lisa Lineweaver, a senior program officer at the Boston Plan. It focuses in depth on only two skills (finding evidence and making inferences) and helps teachers diagnose reading difficulties on the basis of wrong answers. Answers are categorized as correct; "out of place," meaning that the answer is "a near miss" based on a misreading of the text; or "out of bounds," meaning that it is not based on the text. Comments on particular wrong answers can help teachers see where students are having trouble. Are they associating one word with another? "Plugging in" a plausible but irrelevant answer? Misapplying information gleaned elsewhere in the text?

The results come back a few days after the test is administered. After the assessment, the Boston Plan provides coaches who work with teachers to help them adjust instruction appropriately, based on student responses. Teachers are also encouraged to conference with children to probe more deeply into students' level of background knowledge and reasoning processes. "There is no way of knowing for sure what a kid is thinking unless you know the kid," Lineweaver says.

This chapter originally appeared in the November/December 2006 issue of the Harvard Education Letter.

FOR FURTHER INFORMATION

P. Black and D. Wiliam. "Assessment and Classroom Learning." *Assessment in Education* 5, no. 1 (1998): 7–74.

P. Black and D. Wiliam. "Inside the Black Box: Raising Standards through Classroom Assessment." *Phi Delta Kappan* 80, no. 2 (1998): 139–148.

L.A. Shepard. "The Role of Classroom Assessment in Teaching and Learning." (CSE Technical Report 517.) Los Angeles: University of California, Los Angeles, Graduate School of Education and Information Studies, National Center on Evaluation, Standards, and Student Testing, 2000.

CHAPTER 3

An Inexact Science

What are the technical challenges involved in using value-added measures?

Robert Rothman

Every year, teachers in Tennessee receive two reports on their students' academic performance. The first, which details their scores on state accountability tests, is reported publicly and used in school reports on student achievement.

The second report is shared only with the teacher and the principal. That report analyzes the students' test results based on their past performance and background characteristics to calculate the "value added" by the teacher in terms of student learning. Teachers with high value-added scores improved student performance faster than expected, while those with low scores did less well.

Under state law, the value-added scores may not be used to grant or deny tenure, pay increases, or other rewards. However, principals have used the information to make decisions about professional development, and some districts have used the scores in special initiatives. Chattanooga, for example, offered incentives to teachers with high value-added scores who agreed to teach in low-performing schools.

In recent years, value-added measures have received new scrutiny as tools for measuring teacher performance. Despite growing enthusiasm for this new approach, researchers caution that it has limitations. Depending on the model used, a value-added measure may not be able to isolate a teacher's effect on student achievement from other factors that lie outside his or her control. In addition, like inferences drawn from any accountability test, the measures may be subject to statistical error or distortion. As a result, some researchers and educators say, it could be unfair to use value-added measures to make important decisions about teachers.

But others point out that these challenges can be mitigated. And, notes Dan Goldhaber, a research professor at the University of Washington Bothell, value-added measures are far superior to traditional measures in determining teachers' effectiveness. "They're not compared against Nirvana," he says. "The alternative measures of determining tenure and determining pay look every bit as inaccurate as value-added [measures], if not more."

FROM FARMS TO CLASSROOMS

The value-added approach has its roots on the farm. As a statistician at the University of Tennessee's school of agriculture, William L. Sanders developed a way to determine the productivity of farms while controlling for environmental factors. When then-Governor Lamar Alexander was considering awarding merit pay to effective teachers, Sanders adapted his methodology to education. The same approach that could show which farmers were most productive, regardless of the quality of their farm's soil, could be used to show which teachers were most effective, regardless of the characteristics of their students. The state legislature adopted Sanders' approach in 1992, where it has been used statewide ever since.

Traditional ways of assessing teacher quality tend to focus on the inputs teachers bring into the classroom, such as credentials and experience. By contrast, value-added measures are based on outcomes, or student achievement.

In addition, value-added measures appear to correct for some of the inequities usually associated with judging schools or teachers on their students' year-end scores on state accountability tests. Most states measure school performance by comparing one cohort's year-end scores to the scores of last year's cohort. Similarly, principals may judge an individual teacher's performance based on her students' final scores each year. But these scores may vary, due to the background characteristics of the students that make up each year's cohort. Value-added measures are based on the same accountability tests, but they show how much students in a particular teacher's classroom improved over the course of a year, regardless of where they fall in relation to a fixed standard of proficiency. As a result, they don't reward teachers for having a class of high achievers or punish teachers who happen to be assigned lower-performing pupils. "It's a fairer measure," says Jane Hannaway, director of the education policy center at the Urban Institute. "You want to look at what the teacher contributes [to student learning]."

More than 300 school districts nationwide have begun using value-added methods to analyze student data. And in 2006 the U.S. Department of Education approved a pilot program in 15 states that allowed them to use a variation on value-added methodologies to rate adequate yearly performance (AYP) based on growth in student achievement rather than on the proportion of students who attain a particular level of performance (see "Growth Models for Making AYP").

GROWTH MODELS FOR MAKING AYP

Under No Child Left Behind, schools are designated as making adequate yearly progress (AYP) if sufficient numbers of students are rated "proficient" on state tests. However, this provision penalizes schools that are making substantial progress in raising student scores, even though their students are still below proficiency.

In 2006, the U.S. Department of Education approved a pilot program that would allow 15 states to use "growth models" based on value-added methods to determine whether a school makes AYP. While these state initiatives use value-added methodologies similar to those used to measure teacher effectiveness, there are significant differences. The biggest difference is that states must demonstrate that schools are on a path toward proficiency—not just that they made gains in achievement in a year.

Pennsylvania's proposal to the U.S. Department of Education, for example, notes that the state has been using a value-added model for school improvement planning, in which schools are rated based on whether students as a whole have met or exceeded a growth standard. However, for the NCLB pilot, the state developed a second approach, called projection to proficiency, which rates schools on whether students are on a trajectory to meet proficiency standards in the near future. If students make gains in achievement but continue to fall below the projection line, the school has not made adequate yearly progress.

CONTROLLING FOR COMPLICATING FACTORS

Although methods for calculating the value added in a classroom differ somewhat, they generally begin by calculating an expected trajectory for student improvement for the class. Starting with students' prior level of achievement and controlling for student background characteristics that are associated with achievement—such as students' race and ethnicity, socioeconomic levels, and gender—statisticians calculate an expected level of achievement at the end of the year. Teachers whose students exceed that level are considered effective, while those whose students grow less rapidly than expected are considered less effective.

The selection of control factors is critical, argues Douglas O. Staiger, the John French Professor of Economics at Dartmouth College, who has applied value-added methods in medical as well as educational settings. "If you haven't adjusted for the right things, it's possible that someone appears to be a good teacher, but maybe that was because she was assigned good learners," he says. "Her kids would get better test scores no matter what."

Staiger suggests that teachers should be involved in selecting control factors and notes that he has asked medical practitioners to develop a list of control factors to create a system for evaluating the effectiveness of pediatric intensive care units. "Teachers have a vested interest in getting it right," Staiger says.

Yet even involving teachers might not be enough. For one thing, some of the most important factors are not measurable, making measures of teacher effectiveness inexact, notes Daniel F. McCaffery, a senior statistician at the Rand Corporation. "We don't know how many kids have parents who value education, how many have books in the home, how many are in a community that is backing the school," McCaffery says.

In addition, value-added models assume that students' growth trajectories will remain the same from year to year, but in fact students often experience changes that influence their learning. As a result, the teachers' ratings might be affected by student factors that have nothing to do with teacher quality, notes Hannaway. "A student might have large year-to-year gains, but this year, there was a divorce in the family," she says. "The student will probably perform less well than in previous years. The model will not take that into account."

One way to account for at least some complicating factors is to assign students randomly to teachers. That way, extraneous factors will be randomly distributed, rather than concentrated among particular teachers. But such assignments are rarely feasible, says Douglas N. Harris, an assistant professor in the school of education at the University of Wisconsin–Madison. Principals like to match students with teachers—for instance, if one teacher is particularly good at working with behaviorally challenged learners, a principal may assign more such students to her class. As a result, Harris says, statisticians are unlikely to come up with a value-added measure that is free of selection bias. "We know we can't do that by any means perfectly," he says.

ERROR AND FLUCTUATION

Like any statistical measure, a value-added assessment is an estimate based on a limited sample. For teachers, the sample is the number of students who remain in the class the entire year. And like any estimate, the measures are subject to error, or "noise," which confounds the results.

In practice, researchers have found that teacher scores on value-added measures tend to fluctuate quite a bit from year to year. "One year, a teacher looks good; the next year, the teacher does not look good," says Harris. "Their actual performance doesn't bounce like that."

One way researchers have tried to correct for measurement error is to collect more data. By taking three years' worth of achievement results for a given teacher, Staiger says, statisticians can smooth out much of the fluctuation. Yet doing so makes the process of performing the value-added analysis more complicated. Many teachers do not teach the same subject three years in a row. And the data collection is a challenge under any circumstances, says McCaffery, especially making sure that data are collected only for students who stayed in a given teacher's class all year. "Preparing the data [and] linking the right teacher to the right kids are hard," he says. "It takes a lot of care to get this right."

And, he notes, even with three years of data, the results might not be precise enough to make fine-grained distinctions among teachers' performance. "You can find teachers who are clearly good and teachers who are functioning extremely poorly," he says. "But if your rating is [in the middle, close to mine], you can't say you're doing better than I am."

SCALING THE TESTS

Some of the technical challenges associated with value-added methodologies stem from the tests themselves. Like all tests, which only sample the content students are expected to learn, accountability tests are subject to measurement error and can contribute to some of the fluctuations in teacher ratings.

In addition, tests used to analyze value added must yield results on a uniform scale for all grades in order to produce reliable measures. This means that an increase in student scores from a 250 in grade 3 to a 300 in grade 4 represents the same improvement in teacher effectiveness as an increase from 350 to 400 over that period.

In practice, however, not all state accountability tests are capable of yielding such easily comparable results. In some cases, there are few high-level test items, so it is difficult for high-performing students to increase their scores by very much. Alternatively, if there are many lower-level items, low-performing students can increase their scores substantially even if they learn just a little more.

To compensate for this problem, statisticians often do calculations to place student test results on a separate, properly adjusted scale, but it is unclear whether or to what degree this solution affects teacher ratings, says Staiger. "It's an open empirical question how important the scaling of the test is," he says.

And, as in any test-based accountability system, teachers can boost scores without improving learning simply by teaching to the test, he adds.

MAKING DECISIONS ABOUT TEACHERS

For that reason, Staiger and others warn against relying exclusively on value-added measures in making critical decisions about teachers. "It's hard to justify not including any measure of student outcomes," says Harris. "But at the same time, that shouldn't be the only basis for teacher-tenure decisions and compensation decisions. There is a middle ground here."

A bigger question is whether using such measures ultimately makes a difference in classroom and student performance. And for now, that question is largely unanswered, Harris says. Despite the number of districts gathering value-added data, there is little evidence that administrators are acting on this information in ways that would affect classroom instruction. Instead, districts and principals have continued to base day-to-day staffing and instructional decisions on the measures used for accountability purposes.

"You can go through all the statistical gymnastics, and if you still don't have a positive impact on schools, it doesn't matter what the technical properties are," Harris says.

This chapter originally appeared in the March/April 2009 issue of the Harvard Education Letter.

FOR FURTHER INFORMATION

D.F. McCaffery, J.R. Lockwood, D.M. Koretz, and L. Hamilton. *Evaluating Value Added Models for Teacher Accountability*. Santa Monica, CA: Rand, 2003.

D. Goldhaber and M. Hansen. *Assessing the Potential of Using Value-Added Estimates of Teacher Job Performance for Making Tenure Decisions*. Bothell, WA: University of Washington Bothell, Center for Reinventing Public Education, 2008.

D.N. Harris. "Would Accountability Based on Teacher Value Added Be Smart Policy? An Examination of the Statistical Properties and Policy Alternatives." *Education Finance and Policy*, 4, no. 4 (2009) 319–350.

PART II

Using Data to Improve Instruction

CHAPTER 4

The "Data Wise" Improvement Process

Eight steps for using test data to improve teaching and learning

Kathryn Parker Boudett, Elizabeth A. City, and Richard J. Murnane

The package containing data from the previous spring's mandatory state exam landed with a thud on principal Roger Bolton's desk. The local newspaper had already published an article listing Franklin High as a school "in need of improvement." Now this package from the state offered the gory details. Roger had five years of packages like this one, sharing shelf space with binders and boxes filled with results from the other assessments required by the district and state. The sheer mass of paper was overwhelming. Roger wanted to believe that there was something his faculty could learn from all these numbers that would help them increase student learning. But he didn't know where to start.

School leaders across the nation share Roger's frustration. The barriers to constructive, regular use of student assessment data to improve instruction can seem insurmountable. There is just so much data. Where do you start? How do you make time for the work? How do you build your faculty's skill in interpreting data sensibly? How do you build a culture that focuses on improvement, not blame? How do you maintain momentum in the face of all the other demands at your school?

Our group of faculty and doctoral students at the Harvard Graduate School of Education and school leaders from three Boston public schools worked together for over two years to figure out what school leaders need to know and do to ensure that the piles of student assessment results landing on their desks are used to improve student learning in their schools. We have found that organizing the work of instructional improvement around a process that has specific, manageable steps helps educators build confidence and skill in using data. After much discussion, we settled on a process that includes eight distinct steps school leaders can take to use their student assessment data effectively, and we organized these steps into three phases: Prepare, Inquire, and Act.

The "Data Wise" Improvement Process graphic illustrates the cyclical nature of this work. Initially, schools *prepare* for the work by establishing a foundation for learning from student assessment results. Schools then *inquire*—look for patterns in the data that indicate shortcomings in teaching and learning—and subsequently *act* on what they learn by designing and implementing instructional improvements. Schools can then cycle back through inquiry and further action in a process of ongoing improvement. In the brief overview below, we outline the steps in what can be both a messy and ultimately satisfying undertaking. (To learn what districts can do to support this work, see "The 'Data Wise' District.")

STEP 1: ORGANIZING FOR COLLABORATIVE WORK

Ongoing conversations around data are an important way to increase staff capacity to both understand and carry out school

THE "DATA WISE" DISTRICT

improvement work. School leaders who regularly engage their faculties in meaningful discussions of assessment results and other student data often describe themselves as being committed to building a "data culture" or "culture of inquiry." To build this kind of culture, your school will need to establish a data team to handle the technical and organizational aspects of the work, including compiling an inventory of data from various sources and managing this information. You will also want to establish team structures and schedules that enable collaborative work among faculty members, and engage in careful planning and facilitation to ensure that collaborative work is productive. Because looking deeply at student performance and teaching practice can be uncomfortable at first, you may find that using formal protocols to structure group discussions can be quite helpful.

THE "DATA WISE" DISTRICT

What can district administrators do to support schools in becoming "data wise"?

1. Set Up a Data System

Whether the district creates its own system or purchases a software program, administrators must consider:

- What data to include
- How to organize it and update it regularly
- Computational power vs. ease of use
- How to balance access and confidentiality

2. Create Incentives

One incentive is to require that school improvement plans be based on student assessment results. If schools with strong improvement plans and proven results are granted more autonomy, this can motivate school teams to do the analysis work well.

3. Support New Skills

School staffs will need professional development to support a variety of skills:

- How to interpret and use assessment data
- How to access data and create graphic displays
- How to participate productively in group discussions
- How to develop, implement, and assess action plans

4. Find the Time

Teachers need time to work together in order to learn and implement these new skills. Options can include:

- Scheduling a weekly early release day
- Paying substitutes to cover classes
- Compensating teachers for extra time

5. Model the Work
District leaders can also model the "Data Wise" Improvement Process. This may be new and challenging work for most members of the central office team, but it sends a strong message to the district's schools.

STEP 2: BUILDING ASSESSMENT LITERACY

When you look through the assessment reports for your school, it can sometimes feel as if they are written in a different language. So many terms, so many caveats, so many footnotes! As a school leader, how can you help your faculty begin to make sense of it all? An essential step in the "Prepare" phase is to help your faculty develop assessment literacy. To interpret score reports, it helps to understand the different types of assessments and the various scales that are used. To appreciate what inferences may be drawn from these reports and which differences in outcomes are meaningful, familiarity with key concepts such as reliability, validity, measurement error, and sampling error can really help. It is also important to have a candid discussion with your faculty about why "gaming the system" by teaching to the test may not serve students well.

STEP 3: CREATING A DATA OVERVIEW

As you move into the "Inquiry" phase of the process, a good starting place is to have your data team create graphic displays of your standardized test results. Schools often receive assessment reports in a format that can be quite overwhelming. With a modest investment in learning technical skills, your data team can repackage these results to make it easier for your faculty to see patterns in the data. As a school leader, you can then engage your teachers and administrators in constructive conversations about what they see in the data overview. Again, using protocols to structure conversations can help ensure that these discussions are productive.

STEP 4: DIGGING INTO STUDENT DATA

Once your faculty has discussed the data overview, it is time to dig into student data to identify a "learner-centered problem"—a problem of understanding or skill that is common to many students and underlies their performance on assessments. In this step of the process, you may look deeply into the data sources you investigated for your data overview. You will also go on to investigate other data sources to look for patterns or inconsistencies (see "Triangulating Data"). The process of digging into data can deepen your faculty's understanding of student performance, help you move past "stuck points" ("We're teaching it, but they're not getting it!"), and allow you to come to a shared understanding of the skills or knowledge around which your students need the most support.

STEP 5: EXAMINING INSTRUCTION

In order to solve your learner-centered problem, it is important at this stage to reframe it as a "problem of practice" that your faculty will tackle. Now the challenge is to develop a shared understanding of what effective instruction around this issue would look like. School leaders can help teachers become skilled at examining practice, articulating what is actually happening in classrooms, and comparing it to the kind of instruction that is needed.

STEP 6: DEVELOPING AN ACTION PLAN

Solutions at last! It may seem as though you have to work through a large number of steps before deciding what to do about the issues suggested by your data. But because of the

"TRIANGULATING DATA": DIGGING DEEPER INTO MULTIPLE SOURCES

A central premise of the "Data Wise" Improvement Process is that it is important to examine a wide range of data, not just results from standardized tests. Many schools use analysis of individual test items as a starting point in the effort to understand student thinking. In item analysis, you first look at test items in groups by content (such as geometry) or type (such as multiple choice) to see if there are gaps in specific skills. Then you look for patterns across groups of similar items. Finally, you look more closely at individual test items to hypothesize why students responded to certain questions in particular ways.

Schools can then "triangulate" their findings by using multiple data sources to illuminate, confirm, or dispute their initial hypotheses. Sources may include classroom projects, lab reports, reading journals, unit tests, homework, or teacher observations. Another rich source of data is the students themselves. Conducting focus groups with students to talk about their thinking can be very helpful.

When triangulating data, prepare to be surprised. It is important to approach the process with the idea that you will find something new. When the goal is merely to confirm a hypothesis, only particular kinds of data tend to be looked at and the work often stops when the hypothesis is confirmed. Instead, look for and embrace unexpected trends and leads.

careful work you have done so far, the remaining steps will go more smoothly. In this first step of the "Act" phase of the work, you begin by deciding on an instructional strategy that will solve the problem of practice you identified. You then work collaboratively to describe what this strategy will look like when implemented in classrooms. Then it is time to put the plan down on paper. By documenting team members' roles and responsibilities, you build internal accountability. By identifying the professional development and instruction your team will need and including it in your action plan, you let teachers know they will be supported every step of the way.

STEP 7: PLANNING TO ASSESS PROGRESS

Before implementing your plan, you need to figure out how you will measure its success. Too often, educators skip this step and find themselves deep into implementation without a clear sense of how they will assess progress. As a school leader, you can help your school decide in advance what short-, medium-, and long-term data you will gather and how you will gather it. You can then work together to set clear short-, medium-, and long-term goals for student improvement.

STEP 8: ACTING AND ASSESSING

Your school team worked hard to put their action plan ideas down on paper. Now that it is time to bring the ideas up off the paper, four questions can guide your work as a school leader: Are we all on the same page? Are we doing what we said we'd do? Are our students learning more? Where do we go from here? Implementation of the action plan can be like conducting an experiment in which you test your theories of how instructional strategies lead to student learning.

We made a very conscious decision to draw the "Data Wise" Improvement Process as an arrow curving back on itself. Once you get to the "end" of the "Act" phase, you continue to repeat the cycle with further inquiry. As the practice of using a structured approach to improving instruction becomes ingrained, you may find it easier to know what questions to ask, how to examine the data, and how to support teachers and students. You will also be able to go deeper into the work, asking tougher questions, setting higher goals, and involving more people in using data wisely.

This chapter is adapted from Data Wise: A Step-by-Step Guide to Using Assessment Results to Improve Teaching and Learning, *edited by Kathryn Parker Boudett, Elizabeth A. City, and Richard Murnane (Harvard Education Press, 2005) and originally appeared in the January/February 2006 issue of the* Harvard Education Letter.

FOR FURTHER INFORMATION

R.A. Heifetz and D.L. Laurie. "The Work of Leadership." *Harvard Business Review* (January–February 1997): 124–134.

J.P. McDonald, N. Mohr, A. Dichter, and E.C. McDonald. *The Power of Protocols: An Educator's Guide to Better Practice.* New York: Teachers College Press, 2003.

Assessment Glossary, National Center for Research on Evaluation, Standards, and Student Testing (CRESST). Available online at http://www.cse.ucla.edu/products/glossary.html

M. Schmoker. "First Things First: Demystifying Data Analysis." *Educational Leadership* 60, no. 5 (2003): 22–24.

CHAPTER 5

Leadership Lessons from Schools Becoming "Data Wise"

Jennifer L. Steele and
Kathryn Parker Boudett

When delivering her opening-day speech to faculty at Mc-Kay K–8 School in Boston, second-year principal Almi Abeyta hoped that displaying recent state test results would "light a fire" among teachers and spark a powerful conversation about instructional improvement. Instead, teachers reacted with stunned silence, quickly followed by expressions of anger and frustration. It was the first they had heard about the prior year's decline in language arts scores. Almi felt as if she "had dropped a bomb" on the room. Far from igniting collaborative energy, her presentation of achievement data seemed to have squelched it.

As schools respond to external pressure to raise student achievement, the perils of examining data loom large. How, school leaders may wonder, do you convince colleagues that engaging in ongoing, collaborative data discussions is worthwhile? How do you discuss data and instruction without finger-pointing or leaping to conclusions? And how do you use insights gleaned from the data to make meaningful—and last-ing—instructional improvements?

A few years ago, we collaborated with a team of professors, school administrators, and graduate students to write *Data Wise: A Step-by-Step Guide to Using Assessment Results to Improve Teaching and Learning* (Harvard Education Press, 2005). The book offers an eight-step approach to collabora-tive, evidence-based instructional improvement (see chap-ter 4, "The 'Data Wise' Improvement Process"). Since then, schools all over the country have adopted the Data Wise ap-proach. As we worked with many of them, we realized that teachers and administrators who are spearheading the Data Wise improvement process in their schools—as well as those pursuing other approaches—often encounter similar ques-tions and obstacles. So we set out to develop case studies of eight of these schools, documenting the leadership challenges that school leaders typically face during each step of the im-provement process, as well as the strategies they use to ad-dress them.

INVESTING IN PREPARATION

In the first phase of the Data Wise process, *Prepare* (see "The Data Wise Improvement Process," p. 00), school leaders typi-cally face two critical challenges: communicating the need for a data initiative and creating data teams that are equipped to lead the work. The leaders we studied confront these chal-lenges in two ways: by making data relevant, and by giving their data teams time to develop the skills and systems they need to be successful.

Make Data Relevant

As school leaders embark on the improvement process, they need to convince staff that looking at data will not be yet an-other distraction from their work but will help them do that work more efficiently. For instance, when taking the helm of Newton North High School in Newton, Mass., a school with a history of high academic achievement, first-time principal Jennifer Price found herself in a situation where test scores could easily be dismissed as beside the point. She decided to focus on a topic of long-standing concern to both faculty and the community: how to close the school's academic achievement gaps. This helped her recruit a large, diverse team of faculty members to gather and analyze data. Explaining her decision to make data relevant, Jen says, "Every department sees the achievement gap manifested in one way or another. By focusing the work of the data team on the achievement gap, the use of data becomes connected to why people come to work."

Set Aside Time to Build Capacity

In addition to establishing data teams, school leaders need to give team members time to develop their knowledge and to create systems that support the team's efforts (see "Is Your School Ready to Become 'Data Wise?'"). Shortly before undertaking the Data Wise improvement process, Pond Cove Elementary School in Cape Elizabeth, Maine, had emerged from a cumbersome, externally imposed assessment initiative that was ultimately suspended. Principal Tom Eismeier knew that if the Data Wise approach was to be successful, he and his data team would have to think carefully about how to get the process right. As media specialist Shari Robinson recalls, "[We] didn't want it to end up as just another failed initiative." Consequently, Tom, Shari, and the rest of the data team spent a semester in preparation. They took inventory of data already in use at the school, developed a computer-based data analysis system that would be easy for teachers to use, and chose an instructional focus—literacy—that the faculty had already made a priority for the year. Although the team often felt they were losing a race against the clock as time wore on and the most recent test data grew stale, their patience paid off in the end, when their user-friendly approach to data analysis was well received by their colleagues.

FACILITATING LARGE-SCALE INQUIRY

In moving from the *Prepare* to the *Inquire* phase, school leaders often face another critical challenge: how to engage the entire faculty in honest conversations about data, particularly when, as Shari Robinson puts it, "Data can wound." This was the challenge Almi Abeyta encountered in presenting her data to the McKay School faculty. In addressing that challenge, Almi and other leaders we observed demonstrate two important lessons: establish clear norms for looking at data, and conduct frequent, focused conversations about student learning.

Establish Clear Norms for Data Analysis

At McKay, Almi bounced back from her initial presentation and learned to lead productive data conversations by creating a transparent, nonthreatening discussion process. Adapting a protocol commonly used to analyze visual art, she and her data team now present test score data graphically during faculty meetings and ask teachers to ground their data interpretations in objective observations. With its focus on observation and objectivity, this approach facilitates rich conversations and minimizes the threat of finger-pointing or blame.

Conduct Frequent, Focused Conversations about Student Learning

At Murphy K–8 School in Boston, principal Mary Russo and her staff also rely on clear norms to promote inquiry. They have developed a structured peer-observation protocol in which the teacher who is being observed chooses the lesson, briefs colleagues beforehand, and specifies the aspects of the lesson on

IS YOUR SCHOOL READY TO BECOME "DATA WISE"?

If you are wondering whether your school is ready to use student data to improve teaching and learning, you may want to consider four key questions:

1. **Is our principal committed to becoming a "Data Wise" leader?**

   For the Data Wise improvement process to work successfully at the school level, it is essential that the principal be on board. If you are the principal, this means that you must commit to building a culture based on trust, where teachers feel comfortable admitting what they don't know and confident that they will be supported as they strive to improve their practice. If you are a teacher, coach, or administrator, the first step toward bringing your principal on board may be to discuss how the effective use of data might improve teaching and learning in your school.

2. **Is there time for teachers to work collaboratively?**

   Teachers need time to engage regularly in conversations with colleagues about a wide range of data sources. Whether you rearrange your school schedule to ensure that teachers have ample common planning time or rethink the way you use existing common time, you'll want to be sure that the insights arising in small group meetings can be shared among your entire staff.

3. **Is there someone besides the principal who can oversee data management?**

   To make collaborative time most effective, it is critical that someone at your school—ideally *not* the principal—take responsibility for managing the data and ensuring that it is shared

   (continued)

with teachers in a way that draws them into the conversation. For many schools, freeing up a teacher or administrator
to work part-time for a year to create a system for collecting,
analyzing, and discussing data is an investment that pays off
for years to come.

4. **Is there professional support for improving instruction?**
   Finally, if you want all your data work to translate into real
   changes in classroom practice, it is important to think ahead
   about how teachers will gain access to high-quality professional development, whether from within or outside the current school staff.

which she would like feedback. This protocol puts teachers at
ease during the potentially threatening experience of being observed by their colleagues and makes it easier to conduct peer
observations on a regular basis. Murphy second-grade teacher
Tricia Lampron recalls the first time she participated in this process: "If there were no steps or predesigned process, I wouldn't
have known how to prepare or what my peers would be watch-
ing. But the structured process provided an opportunity to focus the observation. . . . That made all the difference."

TAKING MEANINGFUL ACTION

In moving into the *Act* phase, Data Wise leaders face the challenge of helping faculty choose, implement, and assess a viable action plan based on insights from the data they have
gathered. Taking action can prove difficult; faculty members
often have divergent ideas about how broad or narrow the action plan should be and what kinds of instructional improvements are likely to have the most impact. The schools we
observed address this challenge by getting down to the "nitty-

gritty" in their action planning and by helping teachers "keep the faith" when refinements are needed.

Get Down to the "Nitty-Gritty"

When test scores at Mason Elementary School in Boston showed that students were struggling with writing about texts, teachers were shocked. After all, students wrote about texts all the time in their readers' notebooks. However, when teachers examined the notebooks collaboratively, they realized that each teacher had different standards for evaluating students' reading-response letters. As in many schools, a key challenge the teachers faced was defining consistent instructional expectations across grades. After much conversation and debate, they developed an action plan that described exactly how they would teach and assess reading-response letters at each grade level. Teacher and data coordinator Hilary Shea explains that this "nitty-gritty" focus was the key to the plan's eventual success: "If you want improvement . . . you can't tackle everything at once. Getting people to choose small topics is so important."

Keep the Faith

The Data Wise improvement process is not a one-time event but a model of ongoing inquiry. The school leaders we observed in our case studies understand that the work of continual improvement is never done. At Community Academy, an alternative high school in Boston, principal Lindsa McIntyre and her faculty devised an action plan for assigning homework consistently across the school. However, in assessing the plan's implementation and effectiveness, they realized that their initial success in raising teachers' expectations and students' engagement was being eroded by the ongoing transfer of new students into the school, with some classes doubling in size. Some new students resisted doing homework, while others found the requirement overwhelming and despaired of keeping up. Lindsa and her team realized they had to explore new alternatives: Establish a study hall? Require new students to start on Mondays, so teachers could plan orientation activities? The challenge for Lindsa and the leadership team—as for any school leader at this phase of the cycle—is to take heart from evidence of success while continuing to target areas for improvement.

LEARNING FROM LEADERS

The leaders in our eight case studies creatively adapted the Data Wise improvement process to meet the unique challenges facing their schools. At the same time, they drew many of the same lessons from their experiences, based on their common commitment to shared leadership, collaborative learning, and evidence-based decisionmaking.

As for Almi Abeyta, the lessons she learned from her initial presentation fueled her determination to foster productive, collaborative data conversations among the faculty. Two years later, she was able to turn the opening-day presentation over to her enthusiastic data team, who presented evidence of academic improvement in several areas and then announced that McKay had made Adequate Yearly Progress in language arts. On hearing the news, teachers cheered. Then they dove right into a spirited discussion of how to build on their students' progress in the coming year.

This chapter is adapted from Data Wise in Action: Stories of Schools Using Data to Improve Teaching and Learning, *edited by Kathryn Parker Boudett and Jennifer L. Steele (Harvard Education Press, 2007), and originally appeared in the January/February 2008 issue of the* Harvard Education Letter.

CHAPTER 6

Improving Teaching and Learning through Instructional Rounds

Lee Teitel

Principal Randall Lewis stood at the front of the school library, where members of his district's instructional rounds network had gathered for coffee, muffins, and conversation before the official start of the day's visit. "Welcome to Jefferson Middle School," he said. "We're excited to have you here today to help us with our problem of practice. We're also a little nervous, but that's okay. I've told the teachers that this is about my learning and the network's learning, and that we're going to get lots of good information from having so many eyes and ears in our classrooms."

Randall described the "problem of practice" on which he and the teachers had asked the visitors to focus: "Last spring, we rolled out a new literacy initiative that required a radical shift in teaching strategies for many of our teachers. A year later, we're trying to understand what we've learned and what we haven't, and whether it's translating into different kinds of learning for students." As participants greeted the other members of their observation team and gathered maps and papers for notes, there was a buzz of anticipation, much like a group of scientists about to embark on fieldwork for data collection.

Randall Lewis and his colleagues are about to spend the day doing something that most educators have never done: look at classroom instruction in a focused, systematic, purposeful, and collective way. Along with other principals, teachers, union leaders, and central office personnel, Randall is learning about improving instructional practice by participating in instructional rounds, an idea adapted from the medical rounds model that doctors use. A small but growing number of educators are using instructional rounds to look closely at what is happening in their schools' classrooms and to work together systematically to try to provide high-quality teaching and learning for all their children.

These teachers and school, district, and union leaders work in networks with one another and in consultation with our team of faculty and students at the Harvard Graduate School of Education. They represent all types of educators: networks of superintendents in Connecticut and Iowa, principals in Massachusetts, and mixed teams (superintendents, chief academic officers, union leaders, teachers, and principals) in Ohio. They spend much of their time in classrooms, looking at instruction in fine detail. They learn to talk in new ways with each other about what they see, replacing vague or judgmental generalizations ("She did a great job of transitioning from the whole-class lesson to independent work time") with precise and nonevaluative language ("At the end of the lesson, the teacher asked students what materials they needed to get for their upcoming independent work. She took a few responses and released students to go to their desks four at a time").

Unlike many educators who call for "increased rigor" or "critical thinking skills," with only a vague idea of what these terms mean, network members work together to develop detailed lists of what those abstract ideas should look like in real classrooms. They come to agreement on what teachers and students would be saying and doing if critical thinking skills were being demonstrated, or what students would be working on if their tasks were really rigorous. And when they don't see these signs of critical thinking or rigor, they don't blame teachers, students, parents, or other external factors. Instead they look within the school and district to suggest new and powerful ways educators can work together to achieve the student-learning outcomes they desire.

GETTING STARTED WITH ROUNDS

This focused and purposeful work takes some getting used to. Our team at HGSE frames the rounds work in four steps (see "A Four-Step Process"). Before hosting one of the network's monthly visits, the host team identifies a problem of practice on which they ask members of the network to focus during classroom observations. The problem of practice is an instructional problem that the host team wants to solve in order to improve student learning. At the Jefferson School, Randall and his staff had spent a year's worth of professional development trying to weave literacy strategies into their classrooms and were wondering why students didn't seem to be benefiting from them.

The problem of practice is shared with the visitors at the start of the day and helps frame what is at the heart of any visit—observation of practice. Typically, groups of four or five visitors will observe in five or six classrooms for about 20 minutes each. The host site selects the classrooms to reflect the problem of practice. Because Jefferson's literacy strategies were supposed to be embedded in all classes, the visits covered a wide range of classrooms and grades. In another setting, a focus on mathematics might bring visitors to a narrower swath of classes. The observers are guided by the host school's problem of practice. They learn to take careful descriptive notes and to pay special attention to students and the tasks they are doing—not just what students are being *asked* to do, but what

A FOUR-STEP PROCESS

Problem of Practice	Observation of Practice	Observation Debrief	Next Level of Work
School identifies a problem of practice that:	Observation teams collect data that is:	Observation teams discuss the data in three steps:	Brainstorm the next level of work:
• focuses on the instructional core. • is directly observable. • is actionable (is within the school/district's control and can be improved in real time). • connects to a broader strategy of improvement (school, system). • is high-leverage (if you acted on it, it would make a significant difference for student learning).	• descriptive, not evaluative. • specific. • about the instructional core. • related to the problem of practice.	• *Describe* what you saw. • *Analyze* the descriptive evidence (What patterns do you see? How might you group the data?). • *Predict* what students are learning. If you were a student in this class/school and you did everything the teacher told you to do, what would you know and be able to do?	• Share district-level theory of action. • Share district context, including resources, professional development, current initiatives. • Brainstorm the next level of work for "this week/next month/by the end of the year." • Brainstorm suggestions for school level and for district level. • Tie suggestions to the district's (and school's) theory of action.
Network adopts the problem of practice as the focus for the network's learning.			

they are *actually* doing. At Jefferson, the observers were given a one-page summary of 14 literacy strategies that teachers had been trained to use and were asked to look for evidence and patterns of student use of these strategies.

The third step of the rounds process is the observation debrief, in which participants sift through the evidence they collected together. There are three stages in the debrief process: description, analysis, and prediction (see "Debriefing in Detail"). The *description* stage keeps the focus on a factual description of what visitors actually saw—not their reactions, judgments, or inferences. Only after sharing their observations and agreeing on a fine-grained, detailed description of what they saw does the group go on to the *analysis* stage of the debrief, looking for patterns within and across the classrooms they observed.

Groups then build on these patterns to move to the *predictive* stage of the debrief, where the goal is to connect teaching and learning. Participants ask themselves, "If you were a student at this school and you did everything you were expected to do, what would you know and be able to do?" By linking the task and the teacher's instruction directly to student learning, network members tackle the central question, "What causes the learning we want to see?" What specific teaching moves, what kinds of tasks, what forms of student engagement lead to powerful learning for students? This process ultimately helps identify potential areas for improvement and offers clues about *how* these areas could be improved, including the specific strategies and techniques that teachers could use and what the school or district could do to support them. Taken cumulatively, these debrief practices allow participants to describe the specific behaviors and structures they see that cause, enable, or at times constrain learning.

At Jefferson, the patterns that emerged in the *analysis* section of the debrief were clear and quite consistent across the

DEBRIEFING IN DETAIL

During one debrief session, a team of school visitors participating in instructional rounds discussed the following observations from a sixth-grade classroom:

> Teacher referred to textbook and asked, "What were the branches of government in ancient Greece?" "What were the three social class groups in Greece?" "What was the main resource?"

Using Bloom's *Revised Taxonomy*, which they had all read, the participants analyzed the tasks posed by the teacher and agreed that they could be categorized as "information recall." But when they turned to the prediction stage of the discussion ("If you were a student at this school and you did everything you were expected to do, what would you know and be able to do?"), a fundamental—and unexpected—difference of understanding surfaced.

An experienced principal spoke first, "If I were a student in this class, I would have solid reading comprehension skills. I would be able to understand what I read." To her surprise, she found that her colleagues disagreed. As they'd learned to do in the rounds process, they returned to the classroom evidence to examine it closely.

The group eventually agreed that, based on the interactions they had seen, they could predict that a student in the class they observed would know how to retrieve specific information from a text, to listen for what a question is asking and respond, and to read for factual information. Referring back to the *Taxonomy*, the network members then discussed the kinds of activities that predict reading comprehension—activities like summarizing, interpreting, inferring, or explaining. Since they had not observed these kinds of activities during their brief classroom visits, they agreed that the evidence they had gathered was not enough to determine whether students would be able to understand what they'd read.

By the end of the conversation, all members agreed that factual recall was not the same as reading comprehension. This was a new insight for the principal who had spoken first.

This anecdote highlights the importance of using detailed descriptive data as the basis for analysis and prediction. If the observations from this team had read, "Teacher asked questions about ancient Greece" and "Teacher asked questions about the book," participants would not have been able to determine what students would know. It would have been harder to make the links between teaching and learning.

dozens of classrooms visited. Visitors saw the teacher use one or more of the literacy strategies, but they saw almost no independent student use of the strategies. This led to the *prediction* that students in these classes would be able to follow directions in using specific literacy strategies *when asked to do so by their teacher*.

The final step of the rounds process is identifying the next level of work, when network members think together about what kinds of resources and supports teachers and administrators would need in order to move instruction to the next level. Here again, the more specific and precise the suggestions, the more helpful they are. At Jefferson, the visitors suggested that the school be more explicit with students about the goal of having them use these strategies in their own reading, writing, and thinking. Concrete suggestions included giving students a version of the one-page summary of 14 literacy strategies and having them track their own use of the strategies, combined with teaching students about metacognition and making explicit to students and teachers alike that the goal was that students, not just teachers, use the strategies.

ACCELERATING INSTRUCTIONAL IMPROVEMENT

Our goal in doing instructional rounds work is to help schools and districts develop effective and powerful teaching and learning on a large scale, not just isolated pockets of good teaching in the midst of mediocrity. Accordingly, the network's suggestions for the next level of work are not about "fixing" any one teacher or group of teachers. They are about developing clarity, about good instructional practice, and about the leadership and organizational practices needed to support this kind of instruction at scale. Suggestions for the next level of work are intended more for administrators and other leaders than for individual teachers.

People often ask us, "Will doing rounds lead to an increase in student learning? Will it raise test scores?" The short answer is: by itself, no. Although the rounds process is not a silver bullet that will single-handedly lead to better test scores or increased learning for students, it is a powerful accelerant of school and district improvement efforts. Its focus on what goes on in classrooms anchors improvement efforts in the instructional core—the complex relationships among teachers, students, and content. The rounds process provides a key source of data and a powerful feedback loop to tell educators whether their systemic improvement efforts are actually reaching students. And the collaborative learning approach used in rounds networks creates norms that support adult learning and make organizational learning possible.

As one deputy superintendent from Ohio puts it: "The 'next level of work' has become a very common phrase now in our district conversation. We are all thinking more deeply about the supports. Are the supports in place to help [teachers and students] make the transition [to the next level]? Rounds is helping give us that firsthand data and getting us to think more deeply about it."

This chapter is adapted from Instructional Rounds in Education: A Network Approach to Improving Teaching and Learning, *by Elizabeth A. City, Richard F. Elmore, Sarah E. Fiarman, and Lee Teitel (Harvard Education Press, 2009), and originally appeared in the May/June 2009 issue of the* Harvard Education Letter.

PART III

Great Teachers and Leaders

CHAPTER 7

Landing the "Highly Qualified Teacher"

How administrators can hire—and keep—the best

Robert Rothman

Applicants for teaching positions at Blue Creek Elementary School in the North Colonie (N.Y.) School District go through a grueling process. First, a team assembled from all six elementary schools in the district screens their applications, looking at their college grade-point averages, the rigor of the courses they took, their extracurricular activities, and their experience working with diverse students, among other factors. Promising applicants are then invited for interviews.

The interview process is "overwhelming" for the candidates, according to Rose Jackson, Blue Creek's principal. In all, six principals, an assistant superintendent, two or three parents, and two or three students quiz prospective teachers on instructional issues, such as classroom management strategies and ideas for using technology. And that's not all. "If we have the opportunity—we don't do it as much as we'd like— we observe the teacher or invite them to do a model lesson," says Jackson. "That's been successful for us, although it is stressful for the candidates."

The process at Blue Creek is unusually thorough. Because the district, which is located outside of Albany, attracts 200 to 300 applicants for every elementary teaching position, principals like Jackson can select from a variety of competitive candidates. In addition, the screening process eliminates the central office bottlenecks that often plague large districts, particularly urban districts, which in many cases hire teachers close to—or after—the start of the school year and have a limited pool from which to draw. Few schools conduct the intense interviews and teacher observations that Blue Creek does.

Yet even Jackson worries that the North Colonie process may not be perfect in matching applicants to positions. The initial screening of paper credentials might weed out an excellent prospective teacher, she notes. "The best candidate for us might be one we turned down," Jackson says.

THE RESEARCH: TEACHING COUNTS

Although the process of hiring workers is a challenge in any industry, the stakes of getting it right in education are particularly high. A growing body of research suggests strongly that the quality of teaching is the largest school-related factor associated with student achievement. Studies conducted in Tennessee, Dallas, and elsewhere have shown that good teachers can improve student achievement by as much as an extra grade level over the course of a year.

Moreover, the effects of teacher quality are cumulative. Researchers from the Dallas Independent School District found that students assigned for three years in a row to effective teachers—those whose students gained in achievement more than would be expected by past performance—went from the 59th percentile in the fourth grade to the 76th percentile in the sixth. But a similar group of students assigned to less effective teachers actually lost ground over that period: they went from the 60th percentile to the 42nd.

The Tennessee study, which examined the "value added" that teachers provide, showed that even low-achieving students of the most effective teachers gained about three times as much in achievement as those taught by the least effective teachers.

Reflecting such findings, the No Child Left Behind Act, the 2001 reauthorization of the Elementary and Secondary Education Act, requires schools to employ "highly qualified teachers" in every classroom. Although the law allows states to come up with their own definitions of "highly qualified," the U.S. Department of Education requires that, at a minimum, such teachers have a four-year college degree, a full state teaching license, and demonstrated knowledge of the subject they are teaching, either by having a college major in the subject or by passing an examination.

WHO *IS* THE EFFECTIVE TEACHER?

There is little research on the characteristics of effective teachers—perhaps surprising, given the growing recognition of the importance of teaching. One recent synthesis, conducted by Jennifer King Rice, an associate professor of educational policy and leadership at the University of Maryland, found that teachers' years of experience, the selectivity of the college or university they attended, whether they held a certificate in the subject they taught, their coursework in subject matter and pedagogy, and their verbal abilities (as measured by tests like the SAT) were all associated with higher levels of student achievement. By contrast, there was little evidence of the impact on student achievement of emergency certification or scores on teacher licensing tests.

However, the study also found large gaps in the research. There is little research, for example, on teacher quality in elementary and middle schools, in subjects other than mathematics, and for teachers of special populations, such as English Language learners or students with disabilities.

Nevertheless, the research does suggest some factors principals can look for in hiring teachers, Rice says. Subject-area knowledge is important, and an undergraduate major in the subject taught is a useful clue, particularly for high school mathematics teachers. But "advanced degrees don't seem to matter much, unless you pay close attention to the alignment of what teachers teach and what is learned in the higher degree programs," she says. On the other hand, knowledge of pedagogy is crucial. "I would be reluctant to hire anyone with no experience or no coursework in teaching methods," Rice says.

In an effort to codify these types of factors, the American Board for Certification of Teacher Excellence (ABCTE), founded in 2001, developed a test for any prospective teacher, regardless of whether or not the candidate attended a teacher-education institution. (As of January 2010, Florida, Idaho, Mississippi, Missouri, New Hampshire, Pennsylvania, South Carolina, Utah, and Oklahoma have approved ABCTE certification.)

Kathleen Madigan, president of the ABCTE, says the test reflects the concerns of principals and others who hire new teachers. "We had administrators, principals, superintendents, and personnel directors help us determine what beginning teachers need to know," she says. "We were attentive to what they see as everyday needs."

The test includes items on subject-area knowledge and pedagogical knowledge. Madigan says that any teacher who passes the test would be ready to teach. "You learn to teach on the job," she says. "If you have solid subject-area knowledge and professional teaching knowledge under your belt, you're ready to start learning your craft."

FINDING THE RIGHT FIT

Still, some educators caution that such knowledge, while necessary for beginning teachers, is not sufficient and that principals need to look at additional factors before deciding whether to hire a new teacher. "A principal needs to take into consideration the culture of the school and the population of students," says Michael Allen, a program director at the Education Commission of the States. "A teacher who would work well in suburban schools may not do well in inner-city schools or schools with high minority populations. A principal would have to take into consideration whether this teacher is someone who has the skills and personality to handle the kids in their school."

Others point out that principals also want to know whether teachers can work in teams with other teachers, and whether they share the belief that all students can learn. And, since new teachers are fresh out of school, principals need to know if they can be authority figures in the classroom. "They are looking at candidates who have the ability to be adults," says Ellen Moir, director of the New Teacher Center at the University of California at Santa Cruz.

Principals can find the answer to such questions when hiring veteran teachers by looking at recommendations from previous employers. But what about new teachers? For them, the interview process is critical.

Martin Haberman, a distinguished professor in the school of education at the University of Wisconsin–Milwaukee, has developed a set of questions that can help principals predict success among urban teachers (see "Dimensions of Effective Teaching"). The method has been used to hire 30,000 teachers in 160 cities each year, Haberman says. Follow-up studies suggest that the teachers hired through the method perform at least as well as other teachers and remain in the profession longer.

Haberman's approach is aimed at eliciting teachers' points of view on a range of qualities—such as persistence, their approach to "at-risk" students, and the distinction between their professional and personal orientation to children—that together help principals determine whether prospective teachers can relate well to children. "How much teachers know is

DIMENSIONS OF EFFECTIVE TEACHING

Martin Haberman, a distinguished professor in the school of education at the University of Wisconsin–Milwaukee, has developed an interview protocol intended to help principals identify teachers who will be effective in urban schools. The protocol is designed to elicit prospective teachers' attitudes and behaviors and compare them with the attributes of "star" teachers, gleaned from interviews Haberman and his colleagues have conducted. In the interviews, principals examine the following dimensions of teaching and rate prospective teachers as "average," "high," and "star."

1. *Persistence.* Star teachers take as their responsibility the learning of every student and do not give up until they find better ways of reaching every child.
2. *Protecting learners and learning.* Star teachers do whatever they can to engage students in learning, even if it means violating school policy or standard practice.
3. *Application of generalizations.* Star teachers take principles and concepts from a variety of sources and use them to improve their own practice. They also can see better than other teachers the connections between students' day-to-day activities and the long-range learning goals they want their students to achieve.
4. *Approach to "at-risk" students.* Star teachers believe that, regardless of the social conditions students face, schools and teachers bear the responsibility to improve their educational opportunities.
5. *Professional versus personal orientation to students.* Star teachers hold strong feelings for their students, but they do not regard a love for them as a prerequisite for their academic success.

6. *Burnout, its causes and cures.* Star teachers use support networks to help them withstand the inevitable pressures they face from large, bureaucratic school systems.
7. *Fallibility.* Star teachers acknowledge that they make mistakes, including serious ones involving human relations.

For Further Information
Haberman Educational Foundation, 4018 Martinshire Dr., Houston, TX 77025–3918. www.altcert.org

valuable," Haberman says, "but it only matters if you can relate to kids. If just knowing stuff was all that matters, college professors could teach middle school kids."

RETHINKING THE HIRING PROCESS

While approaches like Haberman's might enable principals to make more informed judgments about prospective teachers, many school leaders may not be able to conduct such thorough inquiries into candidates' backgrounds and approaches to teaching. In a survey of teachers in four states, Edward Liu at the Harvard Graduate School of Education found that, while 80 percent of new teachers interview with the principal, fewer than half interview with other teachers, and only nine percent interview with parents.

Moreover, Liu's survey found that few schools offer teachers the opportunity to demonstrate their knowledge and skills: only 7.5 percent of the teachers in the four states teach a sample lesson as part of the hiring process. However, the survey also notes that in one state, Michigan, an unusually high number of new teachers—29 percent—had done student teaching at the school where they ended up working. Significantly, new teachers in Michigan reported a relatively high degree of fit between their backgrounds and the schools where they worked.

The study confirms that giving schools the authority to hire teachers is not enough to ensure that the hiring process works well, Liu says. "There's a fair amount of school-based activity, but that didn't necessarily reflect new ways of hiring or richer exchanges of information."

In many cases, principals may not be able to take advantage of the hiring power they have because they hire teachers too late to be selective. According to the survey, 62 percent of teachers in the four states are hired within 30 days of the start of their teaching responsibilities, and 33 percent are hired after the school year has already started.

Moir, of the New Teacher Center in Santa Cruz, says late hiring does not necessarily result in the selection of poor teachers. "I know in urban settings many principals hire at the last minute," she says. "Folks who hire underprepared teachers say there aren't good candidates. I'm not sure there aren't good candidates."

But Jessica Levin, chief knowledge officer of the New Teacher Project, a Washington, D.C.–based organization, says late hiring does reduce the quality of the pool of teacher applicants. Many well-qualified applicants take jobs in other districts because they cannot wait for the urban schools to hire them, she says. "Many urban districts are receiving a large number of high-quality applicants," Levin says, "but because of the overall hiring process they wait too long to hire, and they lose the best applicants to other districts."

In a recent report, the New Teacher Project identified three systemic factors that contribute to late hiring. First, many districts allow teachers to notify schools that they are leaving as late as August, which makes it difficult for schools to anticipate vacancies. Second, union contracts in many districts grant veteran teachers the first right to vacant positions. Third, budget uncertainties make it difficult to know whether vacant positions can be filled.

The report recommends that districts require earlier vacancy notices, transfer requests, and budget allocations to allow schools to hire teachers earlier in the year. It also highlights several districts, such as Clark County, Nev., San Diego, and Rochester, N.Y., that have implemented at least some of these policies.

Other districts, such as Boston, have addressed some aspects of teacher hiring in collective bargaining agreements. Under a 2000 contract, the district and the teacher union agreed to prohibit tenured teachers from "bumping" first-year teachers from their jobs, curbing a practice that often resulted in late vacancy notices and hiring. However, this limited reform was less than the district had sought and was resisted by the union, which had wanted to retain rights for veteran teachers.

A TWO-WAY STREET

Principals who want to make the right hire should also recognize that the information they *give* to prospective teachers—about their own expectations, about the school, and so forth—may be as important as what they learn about teachers, according to Edward Liu of Harvard. Hiring is often a one-way flow of information, from the prospective teacher to the principal who is doing the hiring, but teachers who really understand the school they are stepping into will be more likely to feel comfortable and stay.

In the end, keeping good teachers in their jobs may be more important than attracting them there in the first place. A study by Richard M. Ingersoll of the University of Pennsylvania found that staffing difficulties schools face stem from the high rate of teacher turnover—some 29 percent of teachers leave teaching in the first three years, he found—rather than from increased student enrollments or retirements. "All the recruitment in the world isn't going to help us retain teachers," says Moir of the New Teacher Center. "They are not going to stay if they don't have high-quality support."

This chapter originally appeared in the January/February 2004 issue of the Harvard Education Letter.

FOR FURTHER INFORMATION

M. Allen. *Eight Questions on Teacher Preparation: What Does the Research Say?* Denver: Education Commission of the States, 2003. Available online at www.ecs.org/html/educationIssues/teachingquality/tpreport/home/summary.pdf

American Board for Certification of Teacher Excellence, 1225 19th St., NW, Suite 400, Washington, DC, 20036; tel: 202-261-2620. www.abcte.org

M. Haberman, "Selecting 'Star' Teachers for Children and Youth in Urban Poverty." *Phi Delta Kappan* 76, no. 10 (June 1995): 777–781.

R.M. Ingersoll. *Is There Really a Teacher Shortage?* Seattle: University of Washington, Center for the Study of Teaching and Policy, September 2003. Available online at http://depts.washington.edu/ctpmail/PDFs/Shortage-RI-09-2003.pdf

J.F. Kain and C. Singleton. "Equality of Educational Opportunity Revisited." *New England Economic Review* (May/June 1996): 109.

J. Levin and M. Quinn. *Missed Opportunities: How We Keep High-Quality Teachers Out of Urban Classrooms.* New York: New Teacher Project, 2003. Available online at www.tntp.org/files/MissedOpportunities.pdf

E. Liu. "New Teachers' Experience of Hiring: Preliminary Findings from a Four-State Study." Paper prepared for the annual meeting of the American Educational Research Association, Chicago, April 2003.

Project on the Next Generation of Teachers, Harvard Graduate School of Education: www.gse.harvard.edu/~ngt

J.K. Rice. *Teacher Quality: Understanding the Effectiveness of Teacher Attributes.* Washington, DC: Economic Policy Institute, 2003. Executive summary is available online at www.epinet.org/content.cfm/books_teacher_quality_execsum_intro

W.L. Sanders and J.C. Rivers. *Cumulative and Residual Effects of Teachers on Future Student Academic Achievement.* Knoxville: University of Tennessee, 1996.

CHAPTER 8

Principles of High-Quality Mentoring

**An instructionally intensive approach
to supporting new teacher development**

*Ellen Moir, Dara Barlin,
Janet Gless, and Jan Miles*

The educational landscape in the United States is shifting. As more politicians call for reform efforts that are proven to improve student outcomes, an awareness has emerged among policy makers and school district leaders that a focus on new teachers represents powerful leverage for increasing teacher, and teaching, quality throughout the system.

The theory of change is simple. Research is clear that new teachers, because of their lack of experience and underdeveloped skills, are the least likely to help students achieve their academic potential. Yet school districts, especially in urban settings with high levels of attrition, have disproportionately large numbers of new teachers. By supporting new teachers and raising their level of effectiveness early in their careers, school districts can dramatically improve student outcomes across the board.

Instructionally intensive, high-quality mentoring programs have risen to the surface as a promising strategy to support new teacher development. The goal is to provide novice teachers with the tools they need to become excellent teachers. The underlying philosophy is that when new teachers don't achieve at high levels, it is not because they aren't trying hard enough nor because they don't care about the kids. Rather, it's that they don't yet have the skills or knowledge to provide the deep, complex level of instruction that will engage, motivate, and inspire their students to succeed.

The evidence is still in its nascent stages. But a number of indicators suggest that when instructionally intensive mentoring programs are implemented well, when mentors help new teachers develop their skills in reaching the hearts and minds of the students in their classrooms, new teachers want to remain in the classroom longer and are better able to help children, especially the most underserved kids, succeed at levels that defy expectations.

However, not all mentoring programs are built alike. The types of programs that have a meaningful impact on a new teacher's practice look much different from the traditional "buddy systems" or "mentor lite" programs that provide moral and logistical support alone. Although these programs have a place in making new teachers feel emotionally supported, they do little to build the capacity of the new teacher to impact the outcomes of kids. An instructionally focused program of support is needed if mentors are to impact new teacher behaviors and practice in meaningful ways that will eventually lead to better opportunities for students.

DEFINING HIGH-QUALITY MENTORING

The following overview outlines the principles underlying the components of high-quality mentoring, based on the experience of the New Teacher Center (NTC) in working with a range of districts. They can be applied in any school or district context, regardless of size, location, governance structure, or partnership support.

PRINCIPLE 1: RECRUIT, SELECT, TRAIN, AND SUPPORT HIGHLY SKILLED MENTORS

Much as the classroom teacher has been shown to be the single most important ingredient in student learning, the mentor is the most critical element in an effective mentoring program. If a mentoring program is to succeed, its first priority must be to ensure that it has identified and selected the most talented mentors to work with new teachers. The second priority is to build the capacity of those mentors so that they can be effective in their roles.

Mentor Recruitment

Like teacher recruitment, mentor recruitment is a key step in building effective programs. There are two paths to excellence in recruitment. The first is to include all high-level stakeholders (those who make, or influence, critical decisions about teaching and learning) in a highly visible communication campaign that underscores the value and rigor of the new mentoring program. This high-level support builds support for the program, raises the prestige of the mentor position, and helps to secure a large, high-quality pool of applicants. Building the cachet associated with becoming a rigorously selected mentor is critical, especially when programs are getting off the ground. The second path is to engage in a personalized effort to identify those who would make extraordinary mentor candidates and then woo these individuals through any means necessary. Many effective programs engage in both approaches simultaneously.

Mentor Selection

Once a high-quality pool of applicants has been secured, programs must conduct a rigorous selection process. Many traditional selection routines identify and assign mentors based on who has time available to meet with the new teacher, who has the most seniority in the contract, or who has the closest relationship with the principal. These practices are logistically easy for school and district administrators, but they have the potential to perpetuate poor or mediocre teaching practice. A rigorous selection process prioritizes the attributes of a high-quality mentor over ease of schedule, contract provisions, or perks to specific teachers (see "Mentor Selection Criteria").

A rigorous program also ensures that the process for selection is transparent, uses rubrics to standardize selection, and involves multiple key stakeholders, such as mentor program leaders, site and district administrators, union or teacher organization leaders, veteran teacher leaders, former or current

MENTOR SELECTION CRITERIA

Although school districts may consider a host of attributes when searching for high-quality mentors, selection criteria should at least include the following:

- Evidence of outstanding teaching practice
- Strong interpersonal skills
- Experience with adult learners
- At least five years of teaching experience
- Respect of peers
- Current knowledge of curriculum and professional development
- History of advocacy leading to change
- Commitment to lifelong learning

mentors, university clinical and tenured faculty, and district leaders.

Professional Development of Mentors

Once hired, mentors must be trained in the art of guiding new teachers through their first years on the job. Without in-depth professional development, many mentors will revert to the "tell them what I know" strategy. This approach might feel nice for the mentor, who can impart some of the knowledge accrued over many years in schools, but it is not effective in building the capacity of the teacher to improve. Teachers improve most when their learning is self-directed, tailored to meet their own individual needs, and based on real-time data from their own instructional efforts.

Ongoing Support and Evaluation

It is essential that teacher leaders come together weekly or every other week with facilitators (program leaders) who can help them deepen their understanding of this important work, collectively review data on new teachers, share best practices, and hone their mentoring skills. Program leaders must also understand what high-quality mentoring interactions look like and must have the time to devote to shadowing, providing clear feedback based on data, and developing formal structures for evaluation.

PRINCIPLE 2: SANCTION AND REINFORCE TIME FOR MEANINGFUL MENTORING INTERACTIONS

Finding and developing effective mentors are critical elements of successful mentoring programs. However, if school officials do not provide the conditions that support meaningful interactions between mentors and new teachers, mentors cannot achieve the goal of moving teacher practice forward.

Full or Substantial Release Time for Mentors

In some programs, meetings between mentors and new teachers occur occasionally or whenever the mentor and teacher are available. Both parties are often so busy with their own responsibilities that meeting time becomes a low priority. Even when some release time is provided, mentors are occasionally asked to take on other last-minute responsibilities (such as covering classes, proctoring exams, serving lunch duty, and doing paperwork), and the time for mentoring gets whittled down. If mentors do not have time to get into new teachers' classrooms to see their instructional practice in action, mentors' feedback will be underinformed and significantly less meaningful. Mentors need regularly protected time to observe, reflect on, and discuss the teacher's practice. NTC experience suggests that mentors and new teachers need between 1.5 and 2.5 hours per week for interactions, whether the mentoring model is full-time or part-time release.

Sanctioning this time is much easier in a full-time release model in which mentors have no more than 15 new teachers and work in no more than four schools (see "Full-time vs. Part-time? District-based vs. School-based?").

Multiyear Mentoring

If the goal is to improve teacher practice and consequent student achievement, mentoring should be intensive and ongoing (for at least two years). One-year mentoring programs can provide the initial support first-year teachers need to survive but are not sufficient to help teachers reach optimal effectiveness. There is general consensus that most deep learning about instruction (through mentoring) occurs during the second and third years of teaching.

FULL-TIME VS. PART-TIME? DISTRICT-BASED VS. SCHOOL-BASED?

The New Teacher Center (NTC) believes that when mentors are released full time and selected and deployed from a central or district-based office, several benefits accrue:

- *Mentor selection and capacity to select.* District leaders can be trained to use a common protocol for mentor selection. They are well positioned to recruit the most exceptional educators in the system and can ensure that the mentors selected have reached a common standard of excellence.

    On the other hand, principals have no shared selection criteria nor a common protocol. Understandably, when asked to identify mentors, many principals choose teachers based on who expresses interest, has corresponding prep times with new teachers, or has the most seniority. Schools with the greatest number of beginning teachers are statistically less likely to have a sufficiently large pool of talented veteran teachers to draw on.

- *Sanctioned time.* In a full-release, central-deployment model, program leaders can ensure that mentors spend 100 percent of their time focused on mentoring. Because they report to a central office administrator and are not based at only one school site, mentors are less likely to be tapped to take on additional duties that may arise at a site.

    In school-based programs, however, mentors with release time may be pulled off task to address last-minute school needs, such as covering classes for an absent teacher, making copies for meetings, proctoring exams, and addressing student behavior issues.

(continued)

In school-based programs where mentors do not have any release time, mentoring interactions must occur before or after school or during common prep times. Thus, conversations about practice between mentors and beginning teachers take place without data of practice that can highlight critical next steps.

- *Confidentiality.* In the NTC model the relationship between mentors and new teachers is confidential. This practice encourages new teachers to talk openly about their instructional challenges without fear of the information being used against them in their evaluations—or the faculty lounge.

In school-based models, new teachers are aware that mentors report to the principal directly and are fearful that being transparent about the challenges they face may come back to haunt them in future evaluations.

- *A community of practice for mentors.* In a central-deployment model, mentors belong to a community where they receive intensive training, ongoing professional development, and inquiry-based learning about their practice with a cohort of other mentors. In a school-based model, mentors (like teachers) are often isolated in their work and have less access to community building among their mentor peers.

- *Mentor learning curve.* Mentors who work all day, every day with beginning teachers are likely to build their skills and knowledge relatively quickly. In part-time models, the learning curve is much steeper.

Proponents of the school-based, part-time model, however, point to some of the benefits of the school as the central point of services.

- *Principal choice in selection and investment in the program.* Most principals go to great lengths to select the faculty and staff in their schools. When the central office hires a pool of mentors and deploys them to schools, principals may feel that it undermines their ability to develop an effective team that is aligned with their goals.

- *School change.* In the central-deployment model, some principals feel that mentors are outside consultants who don't have a sense of the school's ethos or priorities. Mentors coming from an external source focus on change at the level of the individual teacher, and it may take time for change to filter out to support changes at the school level.

- *Informal and on-demand support.* Because most full-time mentors work in multiple schools, they schedule weekly meetings with new teachers. If a teacher needs extra support, the mentor generally must provide it via phone or e-mail. In contrast, because school-housed mentors are on-site, they are available at all times of the day and can provide informal or in-time support when crises or urgent situations arise.

- *Integrated support with the school.* In schools that provide multilayered support, new teachers may benefit from regular collaborative meetings with grade-level and subject-alike teachers.

PRINCIPLE 3: FOCUS INTERACTIONS ON CLASSROOM AND STUDENT DATA

There is a significant and important difference between traditional mentoring and rigorous instructional mentoring. In the former, teachers may receive moral and logistical support that might feel good in the moment but by itself is not sufficient for improving teaching practice. Examples might be a mentor leaving a gift in the new teacher's mailbox or popping in during prep time every now and again to say, "You are doing a great job, Jane. Keep it up!" Without specific instructional feedback, mentoring might boost spirits for the short term, but it will not impact student learning.

Instructional mentoring ensures that all interactions are grounded in evidence and critical dialogues about instruction. Although a strong, trusting relationship is an essential component of an effective mentoring relationship, the focus of high-quality programs remains on advancing the beginning teacher's classroom practice. Mentors who are trained to draw upon professional teaching standards, formative assessments, and appropriate content-area standards focus their support on long-term instructional growth as well as concrete next steps to help new teachers improve their teaching.

An example from an instructional mentoring program might show a mentor coming into the classroom and suggesting to the new teacher, "Let's look at your student assessment data and talk about what strategies will help you address the concern you had about reaching your struggling English Language learners."

PRINCIPLE 4: ENGAGE STAKEHOLDERS AND ALIGN MENTORING WITH INSTRUCTIONAL INITIATIVES

If mentoring programs lack strong partnerships and alignment across the system, beginning teachers may receive mixed messages from various support providers and may feel overwhelmed, confused, and frustrated. Strong communication and collaboration among stakeholders—including school and district administrators, school board members, union or association leadership, community groups, universities, and professional partners—create a culture of commitment to new teacher support and ensure success across the board.

In particular, teacher mentoring represents an opportunity and crossover issue for teacher unions. Although many traditional union ideologies focus on bread-and-butter issues such as salary, benefits, and working conditions, some more progressive associations and unions also are interested in focusing on educational issues that impact student achievement. Because teacher mentoring is closely associated with retention and badly needed support for new teachers, and because high-quality programs ultimately yield stronger student outcomes, unions can become leading advocates for comprehensive mentoring. Programs in districts that contain teacher unions and organizations increase their leverage, and likely improve their outcomes, when deep partnerships are created. Union involvement increases program ownership by new and veteran teachers, improves the quality of implementation, reinforces educator professionalism, and heightens respect for teacher leadership—all critical elements of an effective program.

PRINCIPLE 5: COLLECT, ANALYZE, AND COMMUNICATE PROGRAM DATA

Even the most effective mentoring program might not be sustainable if leaders cannot see and understand where the program is working, where improvements can be made, and what the bottom-line outcomes are. Just like mentors and teachers, program implementers should collect, analyze, and make decisions based on data. A wide range of data used to inform a cycle of continuous improvement can help programs assess teacher and mentor progress, identify programmatic obstacles, and explore refinements to program design and implementation.

Outcome data—information on trends in teacher retention, school movement, student achievement, and other metrics (such as teacher and student absences, student engagement, and so on)—are also critical for understanding a program's impact and for making a strong case for the program's continued existence and support.

PRINCIPLE 6: SUPPORT SCHOOLS TO DEVELOP AN ENVIRONMENT WHERE NEW TEACHERS THRIVE

A wide range of policies and practices in the school and district influences the life of a new teacher: how teachers are recruited and hired; how they are placed in an assignment; how course-loads and student placements are determined; whether and how new teachers are oriented to the district, their schools, their colleagues, students, and the broader community; what resources are made available; and how teachers will be evaluated. Strong mentoring programs work with schools, teacher associations and unions, and cross-district leadership to consider the broader new teacher experience.

INTERPRETING AND APPLYING THE PRINCIPLES

The principles of high-quality mentoring provide a road map for districts to build or advance programs in ways that have the greatest likelihood of impacting teacher effectiveness and student outcomes. To be successful, such efforts require transforming education policies and structures that may have been in place for many years. They demand that members of the education community push back on the norms that characterized their own individual experiences in schools and rethink and reshape the critical strategies that matter for children: distribution of human resources, rigorous structures for educator learning, data-driven decision making, and infrastructure that builds the human capacity to succeed.

This article is adapted from New Teacher Mentoring: Hopes and Promise for Improving Teacher Effectiveness, *by Ellen Moir, Dara Barlin, Janet Gless, and Jan Miles (Harvard Education Press, 2009), and originally appeared in the January/February 2010 online edition of the* Harvard Education Letter.

CHAPTER 9

Standards-Based Evaluation for Teachers

**How one public school system links
teacher performance, student outcomes,
and professional growth**

Andreae Downs

Eric Luedtke recalls clearly his first evaluation as a student teacher. The only comments from the instructors who observed him were "Good job!" and "You did everything right." "But I knew I had a lot to learn and a lot I could improve on," said Luedtke, who now teaches middle school social studies at the A. Mario Loiederman Middle School for the Creative and Performing Arts in Silver Spring, Md.

As accountability pressures on schools increase, teacher evaluation and supervision have come under new scrutiny. A growing body of research indicates that teacher quality has more impact on student achievement than any other factor. Given high turnover in the profession and the numbers of novice teachers streaming into the classroom, the challenge of ensuring high-quality instruction has taken on new urgency.

But the tools administrators are given for teacher evaluation are often antiquated or inadequate. Many principals still rely on an annual classroom observation, during which they match the teacher's behavior against a standard checklist. Was the assignment written on the board? Is student work displayed on the walls? Are students participating in structured activities? Many evaluation systems are not connected to clear standards of teacher performance, nor do they take into account how much students are actually learning. Moreover, many principals are expected to evaluate all their teachers every year—a Herculean task that does not recognize differences in needs and expectations for novice and veteran teachers. Perhaps most important, as Luedtke discovered, evaluation may not offer significant guidance in how to become a better teacher.

"Teacher evaluation in this country is generally abysmal," notes Julia Koppich, an educational consultant specializing in teacher quality and labor relations. "There is no time for principals to do proper evaluation, and many principals aren't trained to do evaluation well." Most evaluation systems, she adds, reflect a view of teaching as a set of codifiable skills or procedures. In this view, which originated in the "process-product" research of the 1970s, uniform methods are presumed to yield uniform results, regardless of the characteristics of student learners. As a result, evaluation rubrics emphasized teacher behavior, rather than student outcomes, and offered little opportunity for dialogue or problem-solving.

But at least one district has found a way to convert evaluation into a conversation about teaching and learning. Koppich points to the Montgomery County (Md.) Public Schools' (MCPS) teacher evaluation system as an example of an approach that incorporates many of the key elements associated with effective teacher evaluation. Perhaps the most far-reaching overhaul of teacher assessment in the country, the Montgomery County model, known as the Professional Growth System, puts evaluation under the umbrella of staff development and uses it to continually increase teacher capacity. The system sets clear standards for quality teaching. Instead of using checklists, evaluators draw on a variety of sources, including written narratives, teacher portfolios, and student achievement results, to determine whether teachers are meeting those standards. It also establishes a two-tiered process for evaluation, depending on a teacher's level of experience and past evaluations. Overall, the Montgomery County approach to teacher evaluation resembles the standards-based, data-driven methods many districts now use to assess and boost student learning.

"I have not come across another district that's done something as intense and comprehensive as Montgomery County," says Koppich, who conducted a comprehensive evaluation of the Montgomery County Professional Growth System in 2004. "This is the best I've seen."

THE "SILVER BULLET"

The district changed its approach to teacher evaluation and education in 1999 with the arrival of Superintendent Jerry D. Weast, who argued that building staff capacity was the "silver bullet" for improving student outcomes. At the time, the district used a checklist for evaluation, a system that had been in place since the 1970s, according to Darlene Merry, associate superintendent in the Office of Organizational Development, which was established to coordinate the Professional Growth System. Under the guidance of Jon Saphier, president of Research for Better Teaching (RBT), an Acton, Mass.–based educational consulting firm, the administration and teacher union began to develop an evaluation system embedded in professional development.

To improve teacher evaluation, the district first adopted six performance standards based on the National Board for Professional Teaching Standards. These standards were incorporated

SETTING STANDARDS FOR TEACHERS

To improve teacher evaluation, the district has adopted six performance standards based on the certification requirements of the National Board for Professional Teaching Standards.

1. Teachers are committed to students and their learning.
2. Teachers know the subjects they teach and how to teach those subjects to students.
3. Teachers are responsible for establishing and managing student learning in a positive learning environment.
4. Teachers continually assess student progress, analyze the results, and adapt instruction to improve student achievement.
5. Teachers are committed to continuous improvement and professional development.
6. Teachers exhibit a high degree of professionalism.

Each standard is accompanied by two to seven specific performance criteria and is illustrated by dozens of examples of evidence that show whether a teacher meets the standard or falls short.

into a two-tiered system for teacher assessment. New or struggling teachers face evaluation annually, while more experienced teachers are reviewed every three to five years. Each group has access to different resources and strategies for professional development to help them meet or exceed the standards. Merry likens this approach to a teacher's using differentiated instruction to accommodate students' varying needs. The district offers courses developed by RBT to establish a common framework for understanding skillful teaching and to train evaluators in observing and analyzing instruction.

Teacher evaluations include an examination of student results. But state and standardized tests are not the only measure of student learning. Formative assessments, such as assignments, classroom tests, or post-lesson questioning, are also part of the mix.

Novice teachers and teachers who fall short of meeting performance standards work with a Peer Assistance and Review (PAR) system modeled on one pioneered in the 1970s in Toledo, Ohio. A seasoned colleague serves as a consulting teacher in charge of several novice or struggling teachers. She acts as both an evaluator and a conduit for professional development, providing tips, support, model lessons, and other in- and out-of-class support.

THE POWER OF PEER REVIEW

Social studies teacher Luedtke, who is now in his second year of teaching, is grateful for his year of peer review. His consulting teacher observed him five or six times during his first year and suggested several areas where he could improve. Once he'd chosen an area to focus on, she would give him "specific tips, not generalized things that aren't that applicable," he recalls.

"A first-year teacher can feel alone in the classroom," says Luedtke. "To have a person come and give good advice helps alleviate that loneliness. And there's so much to learn! I don't know where I'd be without that support."

At the end of a novice teacher's first year, a PAR panel of teachers and administrators reviews the consulting teacher's recommendations and decides on retention. In the second year, the building principal evaluates the teacher. If the novice passes both evaluations, he or she is granted tenure.

For experienced or tenured teachers, the PAR process is triggered when a principal formally evaluates the teacher's performance as below standard. A consulting teacher will review the teacher's skills and determine whether the instructional problems identified are severe enough to warrant the teacher's inclusion in the PAR program. Underperforming teachers who are accepted into the program are then assigned a consulting teacher, who plans and implements an intensive year-long program of intervention and support. At year's end, the consulting teacher also provides an independent evaluation, alongside the principal's formal evaluation, based on multiple observations and analysis of student results. The panel then makes a decision on retention.

Montgomery County Education Association head Bonnie Cullison sees peer review as a way to reinforce the value of teaching as a highly skilled vocation.

"For the last 18 years, progressive union leadership has said to our members, if we care about the profession, we can't say everyone can do it well," she says. "We need to help those who aren't being successful."

Merry notes that in the first four years of the peer-evaluation program, 163 new and veteran teachers were dismissed, were not renewed, or resigned, as opposed to one in the prior five years (out of about 10,000 teachers in the system). Nonetheless, over half of the teachers identified as struggling were able to improve their performance and get back on track.

HELPING SKILLED TEACHERS IMPROVE

Veteran teachers who meet or exceed the teaching standards are formally evaluated every three, four, or five years, depending on their experience. Instead of completing a checklist, principals write a narrative documenting a teacher's success or failure in meeting the district's teaching standards, based on their observations and on student performance.

Beth Daniels has taught science at Einstein High School in Montgomery County for the last nine years. In the days when her annual evaluation was based on a checklist, observers "would check off what they thought they saw, but didn't have to justify it," she says. "It really didn't tell me anything."

The Professional Growth System "takes away the subjective parts," she says. "This is much more detailed, it's research-based, and based on student success. It's made us more reflective about what we've been doing."

Some principals experience the Montgomery County evaluation system as a logistical challenge. Writing up a single post-observation report can take anywhere from one to three hours. Daniel Shea, principal of Quince Orchard High School in Gaithersburg, Md., says that he is evaluating about a quarter of his staff—43 teachers—this year. "I have always worried about the capacity of administrators to do this as required," he says. "Can we do it within the limited number of hours there are in a day?" He says, however, that the evaluations and related professional development have meant a dramatic improvement in teaching.

Veteran teachers are also expected to set goals for a three-, four-, or five-year professional growth cycle, which they establish in conjunction with a school-based professional development teacher. The goals need to be aligned with both the school improvement plan and the teacher's own interests, and should be stated clearly enough that a principal can evaluate them, including targets for improving outcomes for student learning. Teachers, with guidance from administrators, also identify colleagues who can provide assistance and feedback.

"When [a plan] is more specific, we can help tailor resources to help with it," Shea notes. "We can also pair people who do something well with others who need [better] strategies."

TOWARD A CULTURE OF EVALUATION

Both teachers and administrators have found the MCPS teacher evaluation system helpful. In her 2004 evaluation report, Koppich found that large majorities of teachers at all grade levels found the system "highly effective," while 75 percent of administrators agreed that it "enabled me to be a better administrator." Koppich also cited more general results, including the use of multiple sources to assess student learning; increased use of data to drive instruction; and more frequent use of teaching strategies that research has shown to be effective. The school district's statisticians have documented increases in AP and SAT participation rates and above-average statewide test scores across racial and ethnic groups, which Merry cites as evidence of the success of the MCPS's efforts to improve teacher capacity. She notes that these changes occurred at a time when the student population in the district has become increasingly diverse, particularly in terms of class and language.

The next step in MCPS's efforts to link evaluation and improvement is to extend the process to principals, incorporating several of the same elements as the Professional Growth System. District administrators have developed six standards, based on the Interstate School Licensure Consortium, and created seven online lessons for principals and other administrators. RBT has trained about 30 staff members responsible for evaluating principals, and a review panel—a version of the Peer Assistance and Review for principals—has been formed. As with the teacher evaluations, student assessment results will be a critical part of the evaluation of principals' performance.

This chapter originally appeared in the March/April 2006 issue of the Harvard Education Letter.

FOR FURTHER INFORMATION

D. Lawrence. *The Toledo Plan: Peer Review, Peer Assistance; Practical Advice for Beginners.* Toledo, OH: Toledo Public Schools and Toledo Federation of Teachers, 2003. Available online at tft250.org

J. Saphier and R. Gower. *The Skillful Teacher: Building Your Teaching Skills*. Acton, MA: Research for Better Teaching, 1997.

The Montgomery County Public Schools Professional Growth System Teacher Evaluation Handbook. Available online at http://www.montgomeryschoolsmd.org/departments/development

CHAPTER 10

A Guide on the Side

Mentors help new leaders prepare
for life in the principal's office

Robert Rothman

For Terrence Carter, the principal of Clara Barton Elementary School in Chicago, Jarvis Sanford made it a little less lonely at the top.

Sanford is the principal of Dodge Renaissance Academy in Chicago, which bills itself as a laboratory school for the training of future school leaders. Before becoming principal at Barton, Carter spent a year as a "principal-in-residence," or apprentice principal, at Dodge, where he implemented a literacy curriculum, helped draw up the budget, and participated in meetings with teachers, among other activities. He also met regularly with Sanford to reflect on the principalship. Now, three years later, the two continue to talk frequently about issues that arise in their schools.

"The mentoring I received gave me the fortitude to know what I am doing and if it is correct or not," Carter says. "I'm a better principal because of that experience."

Carter's experience is becoming more and more common. While mentoring for novice teachers has been a growing trend for over 20 years, mentoring for preservice and in-service principals is a relatively new idea. According to a 2007 study by The Wallace Foundation, *Getting Principal Mentoring Right: Lessons from the Field*, mentoring programs for principals were rare as recently as 2000. Now about half the states have adopted mentoring requirements for new principals. Many alternative principal-preparation programs emphasize mentorship experiences, and a number of professional organizations, such as the National Association of Elementary School Principals and the National Association of Secondary School Principals, have initiated programs to train experienced principals to serve as mentors for their novice colleagues.

Many educators look to mentoring as a potential solution to many of the problems that plague the principalship. Policy experts anticipate that as many as 40 percent of principals may retire in the coming years. Turnover rates at hard-to-staff schools are high, and the demand for highly qualified principals is strong. At the same time, the complexity of the job new principals face is increasing. In this environment, educators say, the traditional sink-or-swim approach that has typically characterized many new principals' experiences in the past is no longer adequate.

A 2007 Stanford University study, *Preparing School Leaders for a Changing World*, identified "well-designed and supervised administrative internships that allow candidates to engage in leadership responsibilities for substantial periods of time under the tutelage of expert veterans" as an essential feature of successful pre- and in-service programs.

"Book learning isn't enough," says Michelle LaPointe, the former research director of the Stanford School Leadership Study, who is now a senior research associate with the Education Development Center in Newton, Mass. "You have to have a chance to get your hands dirty."

"RESPECTED IN NAME ONLY"

While the current emphasis on mentorships is new, some form of clinical instruction has long been a part of principal-preparation programs. In his scathing 2005 critique of leadership-preparation programs based on a study of 500 university-based programs, Arthur Levine, the former president of Columbia University Teachers College, found that clinical instruction was "well-respected in name only." Among the 25 programs visited for Levine's study, internships ranged from 45 hours to 300 hours. Most could be completed in the schools where the student was already teaching.

Levine wrote that students viewed the experience as "something to be gotten out of the way, not as a learning opportunity." His study found that 89 percent of students who graduated from all schools of education said that these schools "do not adequately prepare their graduates to cope with classroom realities."

In light of these concerns, many new programs have sprung up that provide extended internships under the guidance of experienced mentors, and traditional programs have retooled to add them as well. Leaders and participants in some of these programs say that these experiences are effective because they provide aspiring principals with the opportunity to do the real work of running a school. For example, New Leaders for New Schools, a national program that recruits and trains principals for urban schools, assigns aspiring principals to a year-long residency with a mentor principal. "They're not there to be an assistant principal," says Darlene Merry, the chief academic officer of New Leaders. "They're there to learn the principalship by doing."

CHALLENGING TASKS, NEW PERSPECTIVES

Barton School principal Carter, a New Leaders graduate, is a good example. He took on the job of implementing a balanced-literacy curriculum during his residency at Dodge Renaissance

Academy in Chicago, based on his experience as a third-grade teacher in New York. "He allowed me to analyze student-achievement data, develop a common assessment, and work with teachers to move instruction," Carter says of Sanford, his mentor. "Teachers reported directly to me. I was running meetings."

Laina N. Cox, who spent a year in an apprenticeship sponsored by the Center for Collaborative Education (CCE), an organization that prepares leaders for new small schools in the Boston area, says the experience enabled her to look at school practices "with an administrator's eye." Cox continued to teach part-time while she conducted her apprenticeship, but her mentor showed her the world from another perspective. "When she closed her door, I was on the inside," Cox recalls.

For example, one of Cox's tasks was to lead teachers in an examination of state testing data to plan professional development. "As a teacher, I was feeling that there are so many other things I want to be doing," she says. "But with an administrator's eye, I could see that, one, looking at data was important to the school, and two, it was important to what I was trying to get teachers to work on with students. I was looking at the bigger picture."

Cox also notes that the experience prepared her to relate to teachers as a supervisor rather than as a colleague. "It affected my relationships with teachers, but not necessarily in a bad way," she says. "Conversations would stop. Things I used to be privy to, I wasn't. But that got me ready for my position now."

Mentorship programs can also help prepare students by providing them with models of effective practice. Paul Barnhardt graduated from the education leadership program at Delta State University, which requires a full-time internship with a focus on instructional leadership. He says his mentor's experiences guided him when he became an assistant principal at a high school. "All my teaching experience was at the elementary level," says Barnhardt. "One of my main concerns was if I would be able to manage the discipline aspect of administration. When I went into the assistant principal role, I found myself asking, almost every day, 'How did Dr. Loden handle this?'"

At the same time, notes Sung-Joon Pai, who took part in the CCE program, the mentorship also shows aspiring principals that different leaders can act in different ways. "What's really helped me is knowing that experienced leaders don't always have the right answer and that they usually talk it out," says Pai, who is now headmaster of the Media Communications Technology High School in West Roxbury, Mass. "You have to find the solution that fits your own values and leadership style."

MENTORING IN-SERVICE PRINCIPALS

In addition to programs for preservice principals, some districts and private organizations have created programs to provide mentoring and coaching for new principals. For example, in 2003 New York City created the NYC Leadership Academy, which provides both preservice preparation for a select group of principals and mentoring for all new principals for their first three years on the job.

One of the most extensive mentorship programs for new principals is led by the New Teacher Center at the University of California at Santa Cruz. Under the program, mentors, whom the center calls coaches, meet with new principals at the beginning of the school year to set goals. The principals and coaches meet every two weeks and talk by phone or e-mail regularly. The coaches also observe and coach principals as they go about their daily tasks, such as conducting teacher observations and postobservation conferences, facilitating staff meetings, working with parents, and managing budgets. A recent evaluation found that 91 percent of principals who took part in the program's first two years were still on the job in their third year.

INCONSISTENT QUALITY

Despite the anecdotal success of selected programs, both The Wallace Foundation study and a more recent analysis by the Southern Regional Education Board (SREB) suggest that many mentorship programs are inadequate—even though surveys of mentors and their protégés tend to indicate that both are satisfied with their experience. The Wallace Foundation study describes some of the common shortcomings of mentoring programs (see "Pitfalls and Promises") and notes, "In practice . . . it is far from clear that the mentoring most new principals are receiving is focused primarily on instructional improvement or on preparing new leaders to drive the necessary organizational changes to lift teaching and learning."

The SREB study, a regional survey of principal mentors who have participated in university-based principal-preparation programs, found that few mentors provide meaningful tasks for their interns to perform. Fewer than half of the mentors surveyed, for example, reported creating experiences that would allow interns to demonstrate mastery of key skills, such as understanding the change process, developing high expectations for learning, or providing quality professional development. The report also criticized districts for failing to partner with university-based programs to reap the benefits of effective mentoring.

The quality of many internships depends largely on chance, says Cheryl Gray, coordinator of leadership curriculum development and training for SREB. "'Purposefulness' and 'intentionality' are not words I would use to describe the typical internship," she says.

PITFALLS AND PROMISES

The symptoms of a weak mentoring program, according to a 2007 Wallace Foundation study, include:

- Vague or unclear goals
- Insufficient focus on instructional leadership and/or overemphasis on managerial role
- Weak or nonexistent training for mentors
- Insufficient mentoring time or duration
- Lack of data to assess the benefits of the program
- Underfunding

The study outlined "quality guidelines" for effective mentoring programs, including:

- High-quality training for mentors
- Meaningful information about the impact of mentoring on the candidate's leadership behaviors and dispositions
- Mentoring for at least one year and ideally two or more years
- Funding sufficient to provide quality training and appropriate stipends
- A primary goal of providing principals with the knowledge and skills to become "leaders of change who put teaching and learning first in their schools"

In most cases, the SREB study found, the aspiring principal chose the site for the internship, and half the time they chose to work with an administrator with whom they already worked. The mentor's record of leadership in improving student achievement was generally not a significant factor. As a result, interns may have had few opportunities to work with principals who had proved themselves successful and were likely to experience a limited range of school environments, says Gray.

"It's a weak learning experience to duplicate your experience as a teacher," she notes.

In addition, the study found, only 38 percent of the mentors said they had received any training, and only half of those indicated that the training equipped them to develop the skills of aspiring school leaders. Without such training, says Gray, mentor principals are less likely to provide effective feedback to the interns or to guide them by reflecting on what they observed.

"You can have a very good principal who does things on automatic pilot," she says. "You have to be explicit about why you made your decisions [or] acted in a certain way."

Gray notes that some states, notably Kentucky, Louisiana, and Tennessee, are developing statewide partnerships with universities to strengthen mentorship programs. Such programs are critical to ensure that all aspiring principals reap the benefits that mentorships can provide, she says.

"Now, it's very dependent on the graciousness of the individual mentor, as opposed to having a formalized structure," Gray says. "We want to see consistency."

This chapter originally appeared in the January/February 2008 issue of the Harvard Education Letter.

FOR FURTHER INFORMATION

L. Darling-Hammond, M. LaPointe, D. Meyerson, and M. Orr. *Preparing School Leaders for a Changing World: Lessons from Exemplary Leadership Development Programs*. Stanford, CA: Stanford University, Stanford Educational Leadership Institute, 2007.

A. Levine. *Educating School Leaders*. New York: The Education Schools Project, 2005.

Southern Regional Education Board. *Good Principals Aren't Born—They're Mentored*. Atlanta: Southern Regional Education Board, 2007.

The Wallace Foundation. *Getting Principal Mentoring Right: Lessons from the Field*. New York: The Wallace Foundation, 2007.

PART IV

Turning Around
Struggling Schools

CHAPTER 11

Finding High-Achieving Schools in Unexpected Places

Karin Chenoweth discusses what these 15 successful schools have in common

Nancy Walser

In 2004, Karin Chenoweth, a longtime education writer and former Washington Post *columnist, took on a challenging assignment: find and write about neighborhood public schools that "demonstrate that all children can learn." Working with the Achievement Alliance and using a strict set of criteria, Chenoweth identified 15 schools and spent two years writing about them for a book,* "It's Being Done": Academic Success in Unexpected Schools, *published by Harvard Education Press in 2007. She spoke with the* Harvard Education Letter *about what she found in these schools, what they have in common, and why they are succeeding.*

Describe an "It's Being Done" school.

It's a high-achieving or rapidly improving school that has a substantial number of children of color or children of poverty, or both. In most cases, more than 90 percent of these students are scoring proficient or above on state tests, sometimes less if they are in states with higher standards. The schools profiled in the book include a mix of big and small, urban and suburban, and racially isolated and integrated schools. The criteria I used are so stringent that it is safe to say that schools that meet all requirements are rare (see "'It's Being Done' School Criteria"). I consider such schools to be precious resources that need careful study.

What was it like to do all these school visits?

It was great. As a reporter, I've been in many schools, and for the most part they give me a headache. Schools can be so boring. I've been in schools that do things like make kids practice sitting for assemblies. Nobody practices how to sit in these schools. Kids were learning things all the time. These are really exciting places where people are very excited about what they do. They really renewed my faith in public education.

"IT'S BEING DONE" SCHOOL CRITERIA

1. Significant population of children living in poverty and/or a significant population of children of color
2. Proficiency rates above 80 percent, or a very rapid improvement trajectory
3. Smaller achievement gaps than the state average
4. Two years' worth of comparable data
5. High graduation rates and high proportion of freshmen who are seniors four years later (Promoting Power Index)
6. Adequate Yearly Progress goals met
7. Open enrollment for neighborhood children (no magnet, charter, or exam schools)

What distinguishes the schools in your book from run-of-the-mill schools or from "crummy poor-kid schools," as you call them?

Their relentless focus on instruction. That's what they talk about: what they need to teach and how to teach it. That's the main conversation in the schools. In crummy poor-kid schools, the conversation is dominated by "If we had better kids we would have a better school." I've heard versions of that I don't know how many times. Run-of-the-mill schools just teach to the high-achieving kids. That's the standard way schools are run. The rest of the students they just give assignments to, a lot of worksheets and such. Those schools may have some good teachers, but you can't count on the school to pick up on weak teaching.

What other important things do these high-achieving schools have in common?

For the most part, the principals distribute leadership very consciously, very deliberately. Teachers make very important decisions about finances, such as how to use Title I money; about operations, such as opening and dismissal; and about curriculum and lesson plans. The principals really make the teachers part of running the school.

They also set up the school so teachers are successful. These schools are not easy places to be successful. When 90 percent of your students qualify for free or reduced-price lunch, they come with additional problems that many teachers feel very deeply about. So every aspect of the school day and school practice comes under scrutiny to ensure that there is no wasted time or effort.

The principals in rapidly improving schools are very smart. They celebrate every success and find everything they can to celebrate. They'll say, "We may not have gotten there this year, but look at this. We improved on this measure, and we're really going to improve next year on this other measure." Teachers feel supported.

Teachers *want* to work hard for these principals because they know they have their back. I've been in schools where if a teacher admits they're having trouble, the principal will say, "Well, if you're having trouble with that, that will be reflected in your evaluation." That would never happen in these schools. The principal would say something like, "You know who's really good at that? So-and-so. We'll get you in that classroom so you can observe."

Test scores were a big part of your criteria for choosing these schools, but you say they are not "drill-and-kill" schools. What role does test prep play in these schools?

It varies a little bit. They all make sure that the kids are not surprised by the test format. They do what some of them call "test sophistication"—"This is how a multiple-choice test is set up, how the answers are formulated." Some of them give practice tests, but they are all very conscious about not over-doing it.

Attitude also plays a big role in these profiles. Why?

If you think that nothing you do can make a difference for poor students or students of color, it saps your energy to do anything. Teachers have been told for years that there is nothing you can do to change demographic realities. Convincing teachers that they can have an effect, that they are important levers in children's learning—that's key to changing the way schools operate. If you can do something, that's an encouragement to try. If you can't, then you might as well worry about how long your lunch break is. There are really some teachers who cannot be convinced that they can or should try to teach poor children and children of color. They should not be in school.

Many of the schools in your book are led by wise, even charismatic, principals—to the point where you worried about what would happen to their schools when they retired. Isn't this a big problem in education reform?

I think a weak principal corps is a big problem. There's not enough good training on how to be a good principal. These principals in "It's Being Done" schools are very aware of the problems involved in replacing themselves, and it's one of the reasons they are very careful to distribute leadership in the school. They've spent a lot of time helping their teachers become as skilled as possible, so they know how to read data, for instance. It's not just the principal who understands how to do it. Some are very adamant that the teachers fill in the student data sheets themselves for this reason.

At bottom, a school has to have a good principal, but it doesn't necessarily have to have a brilliant principal. A good school leader sets the goals and helps the staff understand and meet the goals. That takes skill and knowledge, not necessarily charisma.

What did you learn from this project? What surprised you the most?

I had been worried that teachers and principals would really be burnt out by all the expectations placed on them. For the most part, that's not what I found. I found very energetic professionals who love their jobs. They did not set out to make good places to work but good places for the kids to learn. It turns out that those two things are not incompatible, and that was a nice surprise.

Are there some factors that people believe are important to turning around schools that really aren't?

I think some of the structural reforms that people focus on are not all that important. For example, the grade configurations of schools. Whether a school is K–8 or broken up into elementary and middle school is not as important as making sure that teachers know what needs to be taught at each grade level. Similarly, whether a school has a block schedule or a six- or seven-period day is less important than the quality of instruction. At a district level, whether a school board is appointed or elected is not as important as whether the district has a coherent curriculum and a [teacher] development plan that supports the curriculum.

There are so many different strategies that schools are using to improve. How do you replicate what a good school is doing if each school is doing something different?

What I tried to do in my book is give a clear vision so that other schools can say, "Oh, that makes sense, we could try to do something like that." That's my hope. Schools like to do things their own way. Some schools like before-school tutoring, some others like to do it after school. As long as the essential work is being done, as long as kids are learning, I think it's a good thing for schools to invent their own wheel.

If I'm a principal of a school with predominantly poor students or students of color, how do I know if my school is in a position to "get it done"?

The first thing you need to do is get a really clear vision of what your kids are supposed to know and do, and get a really clear look at where your school is in helping them. Then stop all talk about blaming the kids—don't even allow this to happen.

So that means a lot depends on you. You need knowledge, skill, and the ability to motivate people with a vision for where your school can go. Some of the principals I talked to who had the least experience went and visited a school that was performing better than their school and got as much advice as they could. Many took their teachers on field trips to those schools so that the teachers could see new possibilities. It seems to me that all schools are in a position to get it done. The question is whether the grown-ups are.

This chapter originally appeared in the May/June 2007 issue of the Harvard Education Letter.

CHAPTER 12

Urgent Lessons from Unexpected Schools

Karin Chenoweth visits eight award-winning schools and discusses what we can learn from their success

Chris Rand

In her 2007 book, "It's Being Done": Academic Success in Unexpected Schools, *former* Washington Post *columnist and Education Trust senior writer Karin Chenoweth used a strict set of criteria to identify 15 schools with challenging student demographics that were nonetheless achieving academically. In her new book,* How It's Being Done: Urgent Lessons from Unexpected Schools, *Chenoweth visits eight new schools with a significant number of low-income students and students of color and reveals just how these educators are achieving their success. She spoke with the* Harvard Education Letter *about the successful approaches and methods that she believes must be systematized at the district, state, and national level.*

What does *How It's Being Done* have to offer educators as a sequel to your last book, *"It's Being Done"*?

"*It's Being Done*" laid out the case that the work of educating all kids can be done, and that we know it can be done because it's being done in a variety of schools. I received two types of criticism for that book. The first was that these schools are outliers and that it's unfair to expect all schools to be operating at that level. I ignored that criticism. The second was more compelling, and that was from educators. They said, "Okay, so it can be done, but I still don't have enough information about *how*." This book is an attempt to provide educators with more specific information as to how these schools succeed (see "The 'How It's Being Done' Schools").

How did you go about selecting the eight schools discussed in your new book?

These eight schools are all winners of Education Trust's "Dispelling the Myth" award, which goes to high-achieving schools where low-income students and students of color do well. That is, schools that are achieving at levels above state averages with small or nonexistent gaps in achievement. A lot of educators really wanted to understand what made those schools so special. So this is an attempt to give readers a real, practical, on-the-ground understanding of what these schools do.

What successful methods were most prominent in each of the eight schools you visited?

Each of them performs in slightly different ways, but they each focus on collaboration and instruction. They think very deeply about what students need to know and then they teach it to them. And they use a variety of teaching methods—they don't limit themselves to one method. They are always working to find what will work for each student. Also, they all have a very conscious and systematic way of building a school environment that is warm, welcoming, respectful, and geared toward academic achievement. Some have "canned" discipline and school environment programs that they purchase, and some develop a way of operating on their own, but they all work very hard at creating an effective learning environment.

THE "HOW IT'S BEING DONE" SCHOOLS

These are the eight schools featured in *How It's Being Done: Urgent Lessons from Unexpected Schools*, by Karin Chenoweth (Harvard Education Press, 2009).

P.S./M.S. 124 Osmond A. Church School
Queens, New York

Imperial High School
Imperial, California

Ware Elementary School
Fort Riley, Kansas

Lockhart Junior High School
Lockhart, Texas

Norfolk Elementary School
Norfolk, Arkansas

Wells Elementary School
Steubenville, Ohio

Roxbury Preparatory Charter School
Roxbury, Massachusetts

Graham Road Elementary School
Falls Church, Virginia

In your book you use the image of a "wheel" of school reform. Can you explain what that means?

Each of the schools incorporated what I call the five elements of the wheel of school reform, although some use different words and put together the ideas in different ways. The way I framed the elements came from Molly Bensinger-Lacy, principal of the high-performing Graham Road Elementary

School in Fairfax County, Va.: teacher collaboration, a laser-like focus on what we want children to learn, formative assessment to see if they learned it, data-driven instruction, and personal relationship building. The wheel represents the essential elements that produce the characteristics I noted in the first book. None of these elements are unfamiliar concepts to folks who have been working on school reform. But these schools have put them together in ways that make a lot of sense and produce success.

You discuss the importance of systematizing the work of "How It's Being Done" schools so that it becomes the "norm for districts, states, and the nation." What do you think are the necessary first steps in making this happen?

We've started on the first steps, which involve clarifying what we want children to learn so that when they're done with their formal schooling they have a solid basis of knowledge and skill. That is to say, as a nation we've acknowledged that we need to do that work, but we have not yet done it. Some states have moved faster than other states in establishing clear standards, but as a nation we have not.

In *How It's Being Done*, I talk about the fact that Massachusetts began this work before many other states, and partly as a result, they have made the most progress of any state in the country. In fact, their elementary and middle school students are competitive with students in the rest of the world in math and science. Most people don't realize that Massachusetts participated in the last Trends in International Mathematics and Science Study (TIMSS) as if it were a country. The state's fourth and eighth graders are up with Japan and Hong Kong in terms of the math and science that they know. Massachusetts is still not in Singapore's league, but it's up with the big boys. That's a huge accomplishment that no other state can boast.

So we've started this work, but we need to do much more in terms of clarifying what needs to be done and how to get there—and making sure that all students have teachers who can teach them what they need to know, and that all kids have access to the same resources. We still have a very unequal playing field for low-income kids and kids of color.

What is the greatest obstacle for educators who are faced with the task of boosting achievement in struggling schools? What do they stand to learn from your book?

Sometimes it's hard for educators who are in dysfunctional schools to envision what a truly functional school looks, sounds, and feels like. In this book, I try to give those educators a real sense of what a fully functional school is like. I hope it's helpful. Right now there's a huge debate going on in policy circles about what can be expected of very low-performing schools. President Obama and Education Secretary Arne Duncan have called for the turning around of 5,000 low-performing schools in the next five years, which has thrown some people into paroxysms of paralysis. They say, "We don't know how to do that."

There *are* educators who know how to turn around schools— they're doing that as we speak. We need to find those educators and learn from what they're doing. They don't always fit preconceived notions of how they've done this, and they don't often fit into any of the categories that academics and policy makers think they should fit into. They're just doing their work with a lot of skill, a lot of knowledge, and a lot of heart. Many of them have gone unnoticed until now, because they don't have time to toot their own horns—they're running schools, which is a massive job.

This chapter originally appeared in the online edition of the September/ October 2009 issue of the Harvard Education Letter.

CHAPTER 13

The Road to School Improvement

It's hard, it's bumpy, and it takes as long as it takes

Richard F. Elmore and Elizabeth A. City

I n our work on instructional improvement with low-performing schools, we are often asked, "How long does it take?" The next most frequently asked question is, "We're stuck. What should we do next?" In our roles as facilitators of communities of practice focused on instructional improvement, in our work on internal accountability (Richard) and using data (Liz), and in our research, we have noticed some distinct patterns in the way schools develop as they become more successful at improving student learning and measured performance. Here are a few of our observations.

There are no "breakthroughs" or dramatic "turnarounds" in the improvement of low-performing schools. There are, however, predictable periods of significant improvement, followed by periods of relative stasis or decline, followed again by periods of improvement. This pattern of "punctuated equilibrium" is common across all types of human development: individual, organizational, economic, and sociopolitical.

A very low-performing school may see significant improvements in students' scores in the early stages of concerted work to improve instruction. These early periods of growth are almost always the result of making more efficient use of *existing resources*—instructional time, teachers' knowledge and skill, and leadership focus. For example, a school might extend time spent on math from 45 minutes a day to 60 minutes, or might make smaller groups for literacy instruction. Not surprisingly, the improvements in performance that occur as a result of improvements in existing resources are relatively short term. They are usually followed by a period of flattened performance.

If a school is on a significant improvement trajectory, this plateau usually represents a process of incorporating new knowledge into the previous base of knowledge and skill. The school that extended time spent on math might now focus on what the math instruction looks like—how to teach mathematics so that students have a conceptual understanding of the math rather than only a procedural understanding. These changes are, by their very nature, extremely challenging. They challenge teachers' and administrators' existing ideas about what it is possible to do. They raise difficult questions about the effectiveness of past practices. They require unprecedented investments of time and energy. And often they do not produce immediate payoffs in measured student performance.

In our experience, most of the learning that schools do occurs during the periods of flat performance, *not* during periods when performance is visibly improving. Periods of visible improvements in performance usually occur as a consequence of earlier investments in knowledge and skill.

SURVIVING THE SLUMPS

Periods of flat performance in the improvement cycle raise some of the most difficult challenges educators face. It feels

WHAT SCHOOL IMPROVEMENT REALLY LOOKS LIKE

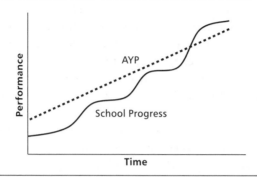

horrible when you and your colleagues are working harder than you have ever worked, when you have accepted the challenge of incorporating new practices into your work with students, when you are participating in planning and collegial activities that force you to move outside your comfort zone—and you see no visible payoff for these huge investments. These are the periods when it is important to develop a supportive work environment and positive leadership.

We've observed several practices in schools that thrive through stages of flat performance: (1) they expect the flat periods and persist through them; (2) they have a theory about how what they're doing will result in improved student performance; (3) they develop finer-grained measures for detecting improvement; and (4) they make adjustments when evidence suggests that their efforts really aren't working.

Expecting the Flats and Persisting

As schools gain experience with cycles of improvement and stasis (or decline), they recognize that the process of school improvement is the process of uncovering and solving progressively more difficult and challenging problems of student learning, which in turn demand new learning from adults. Once the initial gains have reached a plateau, teachers and administrators may begin to focus on a particular set of problems, often associated with broad categories of students, that require deliberate changes in practice.

For example, schools might determine that students are struggling with high-level thinking. One school might respond to this problem by focusing on the tasks teachers are asking students to do every day in the classroom: Are students being asked to do high-level thinking on a regular basis? What do high-level tasks look like in different subjects and grade levels? Another school might respond to the same problem by focusing on questioning: What kinds of questions are teachers asking in class? How might teachers incorporate more high-level questioning into their instruction? Another school might notice that teachers are framing high-level tasks and questions, but not checking to see whether students understand them. This school might focus on appropriate forms of in-class assessment. It takes time for these new practices to mature and become part of the working repertoire of teachers and administrators. Schools that are improving recognize and allow for this time and don't switch gears if they don't see immediate results on state tests.

Having a Theory

It's a lot easier to stay the course if the course is something you anticipated. As educators gain experience, they are more able to explain how what they're doing will lead to the results they want and choose professional development approaches accordingly. We've seen this trajectory in schools' use of the professional development strategy of coaching. At first, schools and districts may adopt coaching because it's a popular strategy and they think that teachers need support around instruction, which coaches can provide. Coaching often doesn't provide the hoped-for outcomes, however, until the school can articulate a theory about *how* the coaching is supposed to help. For example, if the theory is that coaching helps by modeling good instruction and that teachers who see this instruction will adopt that practice, which will then lead to student learning—all that is examinable. Does the teacher's practice change after the modeling? Is there evidence of a difference in student learning? Having a theory also helps identify what improvements to look for in the gap between working hard and seeing state test results, so that you know whether to persist or change course. (For the record, our experience is that modeling alone rarely leads to change in instructional practice, but the point here is to have a theory that both shapes what form your action takes and is testable.)

Developing Finer-Grained Measures for Detecting Improvement

In our experience, changes in student performance lag behind changes in the quality of instructional practice. Improvements are typically visible in classrooms before they show up on external measures. Improvement is not always as obvious as we would like, in part because we look in the wrong places (annual state tests rather than the daily work of teachers and students in classrooms); in part because we use tools that are designed to detect big changes, rather than the tiny ones that lead to the big ones (the equivalent of using a clock with no second hand to measure improvement in the speed at which you can run a mile); and in part because sometimes things get a little worse before they get better. We see this last pattern frequently when teachers go from asking students questions to which there is a correct answer to asking questions for which there are multiple possible answers. At first, teachers aren't very good at asking the questions or setting up a classroom environment in which ambiguity and intellectual risk-taking are valued, and students aren't very good at providing answers that require sentences rather than two-word responses, or at offering rationales for their answers.

Visible measures of progress are critical for motivating and encouraging educators to persist in the challenging work of improvement. Even the most dedicated and optimistic among us will stop if there's no sign that what we're doing is making a difference, or might make a difference eventually.

Making Adjustments

In fact, schools that are improving do stop if there's no sign that what they're doing is making a difference. Having a theory and the right tools to test it makes it possible to identify the need for adjustments. Improving schools are willing to make adjustments, including stopping a course of action, if over time the evidence suggests their strategy isn't working.

THE NEXT LEVEL OF WORK

Sometimes, however, schools aren't sure what adjustments to make. What should schools do when they get stuck? "Stuckness" typically happens when people feel like they are doing their best work and it's not paying off in visible evidence of improved student performance. Billie Jean King—perennial tennis champion and accomplished coach—describes the transformation that occurred in her own career when she learned to regard errors as "feedback." This turned her frustration into reflection, and her reflection into increased focus and correction. Evidence that our best efforts are not producing what we want them to produce is feedback. The evidence is trying to tell us something about what we are doing, and if we listen to it, reflect on it, and give it voice, it will help us understand what to do next.

In our work, we help practitioners frame the next level of work by examining what they are currently doing, looking at evidence of student learning for clues about what is strongest in their practice and where they might see opportunities for improvement, strengthening the capacity of colleagues to work collectively on instructional issues, and increasing the specificity, or "grain size," of the instructional practices they are working on.

It is not unusual for schools to be doing very good work in a given content area—math or literacy—and for that work to be manifested in visible improvements in student performance. As time passes, however, teachers and administrators discover that what they considered to be their "best" work is not reaching certain students, or that performance overall is stuck in the middle range and not moving into the advanced range. These kinds of problems typically require closer examination of what students who are doing their "best" work are actually doing. What teachers typically discover is that the actual tasks that students are being asked to do, while considerably more challenging than those they were previously asked to do, are not at a level that will lead to the kind of student performance that teachers hope for. Or they find that the tasks are challenging, but the work is not scaffolded in a way that allows students to reach higher levels of performance. Or that students in some classrooms are able to do challenging tasks, but comparable students in other classrooms are not. The next level of work in each of these situations is different.

IMPROVEMENT AND ACCOUNTABILITY

As schools improve, three different but related processes are occurring. First, the level of knowledge and skill that teachers and administrators bring to the work of instructional practice is increasing. Second, teaching is moving from an individual to a collective activity, and internal accountability—the level of agreement and alignment across classrooms around powerful practices—is increasing. Finally, the school is aligning its organizational resources around support for instructional improvement.

All of these processes take time. And, as noted above, they do not occur in a straightforward, linear way. Just as with individual students, individual schools really do differ in the challenges they face and in their capacity to incorporate new practices.

Our accountability systems, as they are currently designed and implemented, do not reflect the real demands of school improvement. Well-designed accountability systems would start from an empirical knowledge of what school improvement looks like when it's happening and establish incentives and supports that accord with that knowledge. At the moment, the process is reversed: Accountability systems establish arbitrary timetables and impose powerful negative incentives on school improvement without any grounding in knowledge of how the process occurs. People in schools are forced to invent the knowledge themselves and must often work against the structures and incentives of the accountability system in order to get the job done.

The discipline of school improvement lies in developing strong internal processes for self-monitoring and reflection—*not* in meeting an artificially imposed schedule of improvement. That existing accountability systems don't reflect this reality is one of the great political tragedies of current education policy.

So, how long does it take? Educators know deep down that this is not the right question because it implies a finish line or a summit that we will someday reach. But that's not how improvement works. Some days we may feel like Sisyphus, forever pushing the boulder up the mountain, never to reach the top. But other days we get to what we thought was the summit and realize that still greater things are possible, things we couldn't see from below.

This is why we teach and lead. Improvement, after all, is essentially learning.

This chapter originally appeared in the May/June 2007 issue of the Harvard Education Letter.

FOR FURTHER INFORMATION

R.F. Elmore. *School Reform from the Inside Out: Policy, Practice, and Performance.* Cambridge, MA: Harvard Education Press, 2005.

P.B. Sebring, E. Allensworth, A.S. Bryk, J.Q. Easton, and S. Luppescu. *The Essential Supports for School Improvement.* Chicago: Consortium on Chicago School Research, 2006. Available online at http://ccsr.uchicago.edu/content/publications.php?pub_id=86

T. Wagner, R. Kegan, L.L. Lahey, and R.W. Lemons. *Change Leadership: A Practical Guide to Transforming Our Schools.* San Francisco: Jossey-Bass, 2006.

CHAPTER 14

Is Coaching the Best Use of Resources?

For some schools, other investments should come first

Elizabeth A. City

arrived for my first day of coaching at a Boston school with energy, ideas, and a batch of homemade blueberry muffins. A teacher on the Instructional Leadership Team looked at me, looked at the muffins, and said, "I hate you already." She said it with a smile, but she wasn't kidding. Later I would come to appreciate her honesty, but at that moment all I could think was, "But you don't even know me."

She knew enough. She knew that she had been teaching longer than I had been alive, she knew that I was supposed to help the school "change" and "improve," and she believed that she didn't need any changing or improving. I knew that I had learned some things as a teacher and a principal. I knew that most students in the school weren't performing at a proficient level on the state tests and I believed they were capable of doing better. And I knew my blueberry muffins were good. I offered her a muffin and plunged into the meeting.

In the six years since that experience, I've had the opportunity to observe and reflect on the use of coaching in schools as a researcher, consultant, and teacher of aspiring principals. During that time, coaching has continued to swell in popularity as a strategy for improving instruction and, consequently, learning.

The strengths of coaching as a professional development strategy are well known, as are some of the challenges of doing it right. But even when schools are doing all the right things and coaches have the proper preparation and training, coaching can fall far short of its potential. Instead of trying to resolve all the challenges associated with coaching, schools may need to step back and ask themselves: Is this the best use of my school's people, time, and money?

A TALE OF TWO HIGH SCHOOLS

As part of my research, I studied two small urban high schools, Tech High and Health High, after their conversion from the same large comprehensive high school. (The names of schools and individuals in this article have been changed.) As part of the restructuring effort, the district gave each school five part-time coaches.

The principals of these two schools had very different answers to the question of whether coaching was the best use of resources in their first year of trying to transform their schools. For principal Tony Hobbs at Tech High, the coaches helped him refine his vision and provided critical emotional and collegial support. For principal Paula Martin at Health High, the coaches were people she didn't choose, who didn't match her needs, and who made demands on her time.

Although Hobbs and Martin shared three of the five coaches, the same individuals who were seen as assets in one school were seen as liabilities in the other. This contrast, however, had more to do with what the principals perceived as their greatest needs than with *their* teachers' needs. By all accounts (principals, coaches, teachers, and students), coaching in both schools had little noticeable impact on instruction or learning. On balance, it was a tremendous waste of resources.

READINESS . . . AND HOPE

Why didn't coaching work? As in many schools I've visited, the fundamental problem wasn't the coaching model, the quality of the coaches, or the leadership. The schools simply weren't ready to make good use of coaching. In cases like these, some of the issues may be structural or contractual. A school may not be organized to support coaching well, for instance, by having a schedule that allows enough time for teachers to meet. Faculty and staff may be overwhelmed with fundamental noninstructional issues, like discipline and curriculum (i.e., *what* are we teaching tomorrow vs. *how* are we teaching it). All this leads to a fragmented approach to professional development because there are multiple legitimate demands on the school leaders' and teachers' time, with no clear sense of priority.

"Readiness," however, is about more than schedules and contracts and systems. Readiness is also about factors like vision and hope. A shared vision has been shown to be essential to school improvement. Hope, while less well documented, is no less essential. Hope as a root of successful and improving schools has two elements: (1) the belief that success (attaining the vision) is possible and (2) that each person sees herself as a necessary part of that success. It is not wishful thinking. It is not "hope" in the sense of "I hope you feel better" (a sentiment you may genuinely mean, but with the knowledge that you don't have any responsibility for the actual outcome).

A year and a half after Tech High opened, Hobbs observed that the main issue in his school was that most of his teachers didn't see the need for change. Even if they admitted the school was failing, they would say, "Yes, but it's the best we can do, given the circumstances." Most of the adults at Tech High in the first year of the conversion had little hope.

In fact, the lack of hope among teachers in both schools was perfectly rational. Most of the students had failed multiple classes and had reading, writing, and math skills far below high school–level work. Most of the teachers thought they were working hard and saw that students who did their work learned something, while those who didn't do their work didn't learn much. So why would teachers bother to work with coaches to change their instructional practice if there was little evidence that doing so would make a difference?

THE WRITING CONTEST

The only coaching that was effective at Tech High occurred when the writing coach organized an essay contest for seniors. She worked with students to write and revise multiple drafts, and the whole school gathered for the awards ceremony, where the mayor and superintendent gave awards and the winners read their essays. After the assembly, an English teacher said to Hobbs, "I didn't think my kids could write like that, but if her kids can do it, mine can, too. I want to start working with that writing coach."

This teacher had had the opportunity to work with the writing coach all year but had opted not to. Now she saw evidence that something different was possible. She had hope, and this meant that the people, time, and money that would be invested in helping her develop new skills would have a much better chance of paying off in improved instruction and learning.

The writing contest was a minor investment compared to the school's coaching budget for the whole year (see "People, Time, and Money"). But it made possible a kind of change that all the hours and money spent on the rest of the coaching effort did not achieve.

PEOPLE, TIME, AND MONEY

Each of the initiatives undertaken at Tech High and Health High entailed different tradeoffs in the use of people, time, and money. A look at the rough numbers gives a sense of the relative costs of each approach:

Coaching. Each small high school invested about $125,000 on coaches in the first year (mostly money provided by the district). This amounted to 2–3 percent of their budget, or $4,000–$6,000 per teacher. Spending on coaching represented about half the school's professional development spending, with the rest going to common planning time, meeting time, stipends, and consultants.

Writing contest. The contest involved about a quarter of the writing coach's time ($5,000), half of which was paid for by the school and half by an outside organization; $300 in cash prizes for students; one hour for the schoolwide assembly; class time devoted to writing and revising; and time from the mayor and superintendent.

College applications. Principal Paula Martin devoted vast amounts of time to helping students with college applications, not to mention the $88,000 spent on paying the guidance counselor for a job that Martin was mostly doing. Other investments included $8,000 for a college program volunteer coordinator, application fees for some students, and the time of several outside volunteers.

Robotics contest. The total investment in this project was $1,500 for the robot kit, plus teachers' and students' time after school. For the next school year, the school planned to buy two robot kits so the students could build and test a prototype, and to sponsor a robotics class, since so many students were interested in robotics after the team's success.

SHIFTING THE SCHOOL'S INVESTMENT

When there is little belief that teaching matters for learning or that students are capable of great things, all the coaches in the world may not be able to convince teachers to examine and improve their practice. Instead, a school's resources are better invested in shifting this belief, especially *by providing evidence that students are capable of success and that teachers are capable of contributing to that success*. These initial investments often focus on three areas: students, big wins, and examining data.

Students

Rather than investing in teachers, schools may find it easier to build momentum for change by investing in projects designed to shift students' vision of what is possible for themselves. At Health High, for example, Martin focused on college applications. She was determined that all students would have the option to attend at least one college, preferably a four-year college. Her guidance counselor did not support this vision and, in fact, Martin wrote all the students' recommendations because she did not trust the counselor to pitch them well.

Martin cajoled and supported students in applying one at a time and enlisted the help of an outside organization to provide individual support to students. Eventually, every senior but one (who had already signed up for hairdressing school) applied to college, and all were accepted to at least one college. Martin hoped that by convincing teachers that all students had the opportunity to go to college, she could encourage them to seek the support they needed to ensure that students were prepared for college-level work.

Big Wins

Another approach is to invest in "big wins": highly visible endeavors that focus on student performance and offer public recognition of success. The writing competition at Tech High is an example of a "big win." Another was a robotics competition at Health High. Martin and her teachers recruited several students to build a robot after school. Although the team was inexperienced and could not afford to build multiple prototypes, their robot placed 19th out of 44 schools, higher than any high school in the district, including the elite Exam School, and the team won a special newcomer award. As soon as the competition was over, Martin received a cell phone call from students screaming, "Miss, we won! We won!" Martin described the victory as a "defining" moment: "There's not a culture here yet of valuing academic achievement. Being on the robotics team helped build kids' confidence, and beating other schools showed them that they can compete with kids they don't even usually encounter."

Hobbs and Martin both spoke of building a critical mass of students and teachers who shared their vision to tip the scales away from the status quo. Highly visible "big wins" helped build that critical mass.

Looking at Data

A third route is to look directly at evidence about what students and teachers are doing in the classroom. Both Health High and Tech High tried this approach to create a sense of urgency, but it didn't work very well because, for example, the teachers at Health High weren't nearly as appalled as Martin about the number of students who received failing grades.

So Martin took a different tack. She changed the grading policy so that students could not get a grade below C– at the end of a quarter. Any student whose average was below that received an "incomplete" and was required to make up the work. Teachers were surprised to see that most students actually completed the work they needed to move from an incomplete to at least a C–.

In a situation where there is little belief that something different is possible, data may work better to show something different *after* it happens than to show that something *needs* to happen.

In short, school leaders should work on generating demand for professional development before investing heavily in instructional improvement. Small investments can catalyze shifts in hope that ripple through schools, helping students and teachers see not only that something different is possible, but that it is possible *for them* and *because of them*. This is a process that can take quite a bit of time—especially in tumultuous circumstances like those faced by Tech High and Health High in the first year after conversion. Coaches can sometimes be instrumental in shifting hope—as happened in the Tech High writing contest—but it may make sense to think about cultivating the conditions for coaching first before deploying this potentially rich resource.

And that teacher I met at the Boston school on my first day of coaching? By the end of that year we agreed on the need for change and she was taking a leading role in that change, though she trusted her colleagues more than coaches to help her with her own practice. Lots of listening got me further with her than did my blueberry muffins. But as with all improvement, it's a combination of factors that lead to success, and the muffins didn't hurt.

This chapter is adapted from Resourceful Leadership: Tradeoffs and Tough Decisions on the Road to School Improvement, *by Elizabeth A. City (Harvard Education Press, 2008), and originally appeared in the September/October 2007 issue of the* Harvard Education Letter.

CHAPTER 15

Four Central Dilemmas of Struggling Schools

The starting points for a developmental approach to intervention

D. Brent Stephens

There is an emerging crisis of school accountability in this country. Having passed beyond the arguments about whether schools should be held accountable at all, we're trying to figure out what to do with the thousands of schools that aren't good enough. Included in this group are schools that are persistently dysfunctional, along with many others that truly have gotten better, but not with the speed demanded by federal regulations. For a host of reasons, these schools haven't converted the labels and sanctions imposed by states and districts under the No Child Left Behind Act into any dramatic leaps in student learning. They haven't capitalized on the new performance data available to them. The new crisis—the most recent in a long series of urgent calls for reform—centers on how to fix this underperformance.

Time and again, state accountability and intervention in low-performing schools collides with the realities of the established culture and relationships in these schools. In some cases, this collision appears to bring about promising new practices, or at least helps set in place the conditions that might lead to sustained improvement. In others, the collision is like a powerful wave rolling to its quiet conclusion on a long beach. After the wave's energy is dissipated, the beach remains unchanged; the low-performing school retains its most persistent, limiting features.

If there is a single variable missing from current intervention systems, it's the effort to nurture a *developmental strategy* within each school. Indeed, there's no attention at all to the organizational development that might reasonably occur over time for most schools. A far smarter strategy for a low-performing school would consistently guide a principal and teacher-leaders to understand their school in terms of the general pattern of growth for similar schools, and then provide ongoing support so that the educators could make more informed decisions about which improvement activities are most likely to move the school from one developmental stage to the next (see "The Developmental Stages of Improving Schools."). The alternative to helping schools establish their own developmental strategy is many more years of the hunt-and-peck improvement work that the current system produces in such abundance.

To improve low-performing schools more effectively and efficiently, intervention support must prepare a specific developmental profile of each of its target schools. In particular, a meaningful developmental profile will evaluate each school's response to four key dilemmas the school must address to realize sustained improvement. Each of these dilemmas relates to the tug between change and stability.

THE DEVELOPMENTAL STAGES
OF IMPROVING SCHOOLS

The stages of school improvement provide a useful framework for a school's developmental profile. These five stages should be thought of flexibly, and primarily as a means of guidance as schools begin to ask, "Where are we now in our development, and what impact might the decisions we make now have on our ability to develop ourselves?"

Stage 1: Emotional Reactions and Questions about Responsibility. This period is defined by disbelief and real questions about the legitimacy of either the measure by which the school is judged or the sanctions it must face. The successful navigation of this stage requires that teachers feel that their concerns are heard and, as much as possible, addressed in concrete terms.

Stage 2: Administrative Responses to the Crisis. Administrators in many low-performing schools begin by "reaching for the low-hanging fruit"—e.g., starting remedial programs, creating pacing guides. These administrative actions can help set the stage for cultural change: to move teachers toward a vision of collegiality and mutual professional obligation.

Stage 3: Voluntarism. At this stage, some teachers—the school's teacher-leaders and a handful of others—are apt to become involved in projects that might have an impact on the *instructional core* of the school, that is, the curriculum, instruction, and assessment at the heart of teachers' ability to increase student learning. A new level of trust takes hold among most teachers, and pockets of more proficient instruction begin to take hold.

(continued)

Stage 4: Universalism and School Identity. In this stage, clear expectations are held universally, and broad implementation of, and fidelity to, the school's instructional programs are no longer issues. Teachers identify with their school, and everyone in the building can express in considerable detail the school's particular way of going about their work.

Stage 5: Internal Accountability and Sustained Growth. The end game for schools, low-performing or otherwise, is this: that all teachers agree to and frequently enact a common understanding of powerful teaching practice and learn together so that this understanding is adaptive, conscious, and expanding.

It's important to note that schools don't pass on their own from one stage to the next in stepwise fashion, always in advance; a single school can possess features of several stages at once. The central idea here is that these stages exist, that they have describable characteristics, and that intervention policy should be explicit in its intent to coach schools—through tough dilemmas, crises, and moments of great uncertainty—from one stage to the next as efficiently as possible.

DEVELOPMENTAL DILEMMA #1: THE ATTRIBUTION OF CAUSE

In many struggling schools, staff members and principals grapple heavily with the source of the problems highlighted in their school's performance data. For the teachers at Stoddard Middle School[1], for example, low performance was about the decimation of the city's industrial base, the slow slide of civility among their students, and disengaged families and their

---

1. The names of the schools mentioned in this article—all urban schools in Massachusetts—are pseudonyms.

rough-and-tumble kids. The hallways were a mess, the staff said, because the tumult came from home. Students were impolite, disaffected, and barely engaged because they had been raised this way. The internal workings of the school weren't much a part of the conversation either in the teachers' lounge or in the school's leadership team meetings.

This external-internal dynamic will be familiar to anyone who spends much time in schools. After all, it's far easier to strike up a conversation with a teacher about the infelicities of our popular culture than it is to inquire about the effect of a particular teaching strategy. Even if this dynamic is familiar, intervention design cannot afford to ignore it. The manner in which a school describes the source of its poor performance is a telling indicator of its location on the trajectory toward internal accountability. Because this dilemma is so powerful for teachers—causing so many teachers to feel blamed, then burned, and ultimately hostile to all external help—the attribution of cause is the first place to begin in assessing the internal workings of a school targeted for intervention.

As a starting point for creating a developmental profile for a low-performing school, support providers should consider how responsibility is defined by the educators and administrators they hope to help. Intervention design should include the answers to a few important questions. For example, how do teachers describe what's going on with the school's poor performance? Is this description internal or external, or some combination of both? Is there consensus or variability among teachers? And what is the relative level of offense among teachers who feel impugned by their school's accountability label?

The importance of these questions is not to find teachers who don't see the value of getting help or view themselves as key to the success of their students. Every low-performing school probably has a few teachers who feel this way. What's important is that the school leaders have regular opportunities to work with support providers who clearly understand this dynamic and can help them strategically and efficiently improve the faculty's overall sense of responsibility and efficacy.

DEVELOPMENTAL DILEMMA #2: THE CONTROL OF INSTRUCTION

This dilemma centers on the degree to which school leaders, or leadership teams, assume central control of curriculum, instruction, and assessment. In Connington Elementary School, the principal took to the hallways with a teaching checklist of his own design; in Tanner K–8 School, the principal simply encouraged teachers to avoid the "same old, same old." Control of the instructional process is a hot-button issue just as likely to elicit strong reactions from teachers as is the question of who's to blame for low performance.

Like the attribution of cause, the dilemma about control over instruction has the potential to derail local efforts at improvement and can cost schools years in unnecessary and damaging infighting. But it hasn't yet figured into intervention design.

What questions should support providers ask to assemble a useful developmental profile related to the dilemma of instructional control? First, they should know where a low-performing school has been, what its history of distributed leadership has been, and what questions about instruction it has considered. Has it taken on any substantive issues related to teaching and learning? Has it mostly followed the lead of its district? Has its attention been close to the classroom and what teachers do during the instructional day, or has it been focused on remediation, after-school programs, or other extracurricular activities?

On a related tack, it's also important for support providers to learn about the extent of instructional expertise at the school. What are the principal's capacities for leading instructional change? How are teachers situated in this regard? And district staff?

In effect, collecting information about this key developmental dilemma means asking some questions—probably no more than good teachers ask about their class at the beginning of a school year, and probably about no larger a group of people than an average class of students. It's important because school leaders need explicit support to understand the opportunities and pitfalls of this dilemma and how it can be managed in support of incrementally more distributed leadership.

DEVELOPMENTAL DILEMMA #3: THE LOCATION OF THE RESPONSE TO INTERVENTION

Shot through the stories of struggling schools are fights about where and how to respond to state intervention requirements. How close will schools' improvement efforts get to teachers' classrooms? How vigorously will schools insist on uniform, high-quality implementation? The tug is often toward efforts located outside the classroom—in the hallways, on the playground, or after school. These are areas of relative comfort for most schools, and incursions by the principal or leadership team into the territory of individual teachers—like those initiated by Connington's principal—are usually greeted with some form of pushing back.

This well-described dilemma can be heard in the ongoing concerns among teachers about academic freedom or their complaints about unscheduled observations and evaluation by principals. From the perspective of change agents, this is about the unjustifiable privacy of classroom practice; from the perspective of many teachers, including those who work in low-performing schools, this is about autonomy, professional discretion, and protecting the hard-won right to do right by kids.

As they assemble a developmental profile of each school, intervention support providers should ask what efforts the school is making so far. Are these efforts related to change in the class-room and to improvements in curriculum, instruction, and assessment? Or are these efforts more concentrated on school-wide features like extracurricular programs or school climate? If the school is attempting to improve classroom processes, how much of this effort relates to instruction, which is the most private, most skill-based of the three areas listed above?

In addition, it's worth learning what mechanisms the school uses for understanding the extent and quality of its implementation. Fundamentally, can the leaders of the school say with any accuracy how many teachers are implementing its classroom initiatives, how well these initiatives are being enacted, and, more challenging yet, how this implementation is affecting student learning?

By asking these questions—and helping school leaders realize the dilemmas involved in the answers—support providers give the leaders a glimpse into the working of their own schools. These questions frame a larger set of possibilities, in the same way that pulling back to a full map gives context to a magnified location. To ask whether a school knows how many teachers are implementing an instructional initiative, and how well they are doing so, is not just a powerful suggestion about what can and should happen. It's the beginning of a conversation, which so far has been absent in intervention design, about how best to get there.

DEVELOPMENTAL DILEMMA #4: THE DEFINITION OF THE CHALLENGE

The challenge facing low-performing schools lies between two poles. On one pole, the challenge may be viewed as one of compliance with state requirements; on the other, the task may be defined as a matter of professional learning.

At one end of this continuum, teachers and principals may talk openly about the need to follow the guidelines of the state, even if they disagree with them. "There's no point in resisting," teachers at Stoddard Middle School said to their colleagues, "so let's just get the work over with." On the other end of the continuum, teachers and principals may express their own need to learn new skills to support students to achieve. Here, on the professional-learning end of the continuum, is where research has shown that schools have the best shot at sustained growth. This is internal accountability, when teachers themselves adopt the disposition of learners and then hold their colleagues accountable for reaching increasingly rich levels of practice and inquiry.

Clearly, most low-performing schools are not self-actualized learning machines. They are somewhere between the self-defeating, self-comforting stance of the compliance orientation and some form of organized professional learning. Where they are on this continuum matters, though, just as it matters that everyone involved in supporting the school has explicit knowledge that this continuum exists. If the goal is to guide schools toward internal accountability and to avoid the traps of the compliance-oriented response, doesn't it make sense that these two things have names?

In order to assess how a school manages the dilemma of compliance versus professional learning, it's important to have a conversation about the principal's own orientation toward this dilemma. It's also important to know how teachers talk about this, and district office staff as well. How do central office demands reinforce the compliance orientation? How is the teachers' union oriented to this question?

These four developmental dilemmas, alone or in combination, very often create significant drag against forward motion. None of these dilemmas is easily resolved or managed, and most schools face them without the advantage of either having them made explicit or receiving any ongoing guidance. This isolation lies at the core of a system in which positive

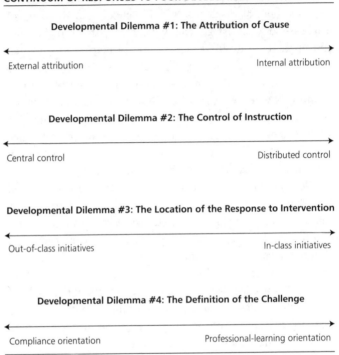

CONTINUUM OF RESPONSES TO FOUR DEVELOPMENTAL DILEMMAS

Developmental Dilemma #1: The Attribution of Cause

External attribution   Internal attribution

Developmental Dilemma #2: The Control of Instruction

Central control   Distributed control

Developmental Dilemma #3: The Location of the Response to Intervention

Out-of-class initiatives   In-class initiatives

Developmental Dilemma #4: The Definition of the Challenge

Compliance orientation   Professional-learning orientation

results, even on paper, appear to be wildly improbable. Out in the real world, you can see the slow progress we're making.

Figure 1 shows what the continuum of responses to each of these four developmental dilemmas might look like. Keep in mind that with each of these dilemmas, the gravitational pull is decidedly toward the left—toward comfort, toward simplicity, toward privacy, and away from conflict. This tug toward comfort and privacy is only sometimes explicit. More often, it is something that principals feel compellingly based on their longtime experience with the way things are in schools, with what teachers like and don't like. These are, by and large, self-reinforcing rules.

Using these dilemmas to assess the developmental orientation of individual schools can help bridge the gap between low-performing schools and the central office apparatus that is, in theory, supposed to provide support. Today, districts get no help in trying to view their schools in a developmental way. There's nothing to insist that this happen.

By considering the predictable dilemmas of schools, this work repositions both district and school; the conversation can pull both toward mutual understanding and support, instead of the more familiar relationship of central office dictates and deep cynicism down in the trenches. When both school and district participate in developing an honest portrait of each school, there's the chance for forming a joint understanding of the challenges and potential in each school. This starting point for the meaningful differentiation of support is what many low-performing schools urgently need.

This article is adapted from Improving Struggling Schools: A Developmental Approach to Intervention, *by D. Brent Stephens (Harvard Education Press, 2010), and originally appeared in the online edition of the March/April 2010 issue of the* Harvard Education Letter.

FOR FURTHER INFORMATION

A. Calkins, W. Guenther, G. Belfiore, and D. Lash. *The Turnaround Challenge: New Research, Recommendations, and a Partnership Framework for States and School Districts.* Boston, MA: Mass Insight Education and Research Institute, 2007. Available online at http://www.massinsight.org/turnaround/reports.aspx

Center on Education Policy. *Moving Beyond Identification: Assisting Schools in Improvement.* Washington, DC: Center on Education Policy, July 2007.

R. Elmore. *School Reform from the Inside Out: Policy, Practice, and Performance.* Cambridge, MA: Harvard Education Press, 2004.

J. Gray. *Causing Concern but Improving: A Review of Schools' Experiences*. London: Department for Education and Employment Research, 2000. Available online at www.standards.dfes.gov.uk/

National Governors Association Center for Best Practices. *Reaching New Heights: Turning Around Low-Performing Schools—A Guide for Governors*. Washington, DC: National Governors Association Center for Best Practices, 2003. Available online at www.nga.org/cda/files/0803REACHING.PDF

CHAPTER 16

Charters and Unions

What's the future for this unorthodox relationship?

Alexander Russo

N early two years ago, Spanish teacher Emily Mueller was dismayed to learn that her charter high school, Northtown Academy in Chicago, was asking teachers to teach six classes instead of five.

There was no real discussion between teachers and administrators about alternative solutions, according to Mueller. There was no pay increase attached to the increased workload, either. The unilateral, unpaid workload increase "just didn't seem sustainable," she says.

But Mueller didn't want to leave the school, one of three chartered by an organization called Chicago International Charter School and operated by an organization called Civitas Schools. So she and a handful of colleagues did something that only a few charter school teachers have done: they began the long, difficult, but ultimately successful push to join the Illinois Federation of Teachers and negotiate a contract that now represents roughly 140 teachers at the three schools.

Over the past year and a half, unionized charter schools have popped up in several big cities around the country. In several cases such as Mueller's, charter school teachers have initiated organizing campaigns to address the challenging working conditions, low pay, and top-down management structures of some charter schools. Teachers at four Accelerated School campuses in Los Angeles joined United Teachers Los Angeles (UTLA) last year. Teachers at KIPP: AMP in Brooklyn, N.Y., voted to join the United Federation of Teachers (UFT). And in September 2009, the Conservatory Lab Charter School in Boston, Mass., began negotiating what will be the first charter-union contract with AFT Massachusetts.

Not all union organizing in charter schools occurs from the bottom up. Some charter operators have insisted on working with unionized teachers from the start. Green Dot Public Schools, a well-known charter school management organization, works with teachers affiliated with the California Teachers Association in Los Angeles and the UFT in New York City. A Chicago-based school management organization called Union Park has recently been approved to open a new, unionized charter school based on the Talent Development model in September 2010.

Some states like Wisconsin, Minnesota, and Maryland require all charters to be part of a district's union contract. Other states, like New York and California, have requirements that vary according to school size and development process. New York requires unionization for charter schools that open with more than 250 students. California requires schools that "convert" from district schools to charter status be unionized.

There is no ready agreement on the number of unionized charters among the estimated 5,000 charter schools nationwide. The AFT says it has organized 80 schools. The National Education Association estimates that it works with roughly 200. The National Alliance for Public Charter Schools says that the total number is somewhere below 500.

Some school reformers and union leaders are looking to unionized charters as the wave of the future. However, many charter school proponents see unionization as no more than a problematic distraction. Whether the Obama administration will take steps to support this hybrid, whether the number of unionized charters will increase, and how well they will perform over time remains to be seen.

A NEW PATH FOR CHARTER SCHOOLS

For proponents like Green Dot founder Steve Barr, bridging the gap between charter schools and teacher unions is an obvious way to make rapid change without alienating powerful unions. "I don't think you're going to change a public education system that's 100 percent unionized with nonunion labor," Barr says.

For some labor leaders, unionized charters offer the prospect of increasing union membership in a small but fast-growing sector. Even more important, perhaps, they demonstrate labor's willingness to innovate. Referring to the Chicago contract covering three charter schools, AFT president Randi Weingarten says, "This contract is a great example of how charter schools can be incubators for innovative reforms and good labor-management practices."

Weingarten calls unionization a "new path" for charter schools. She speaks frequently about how charter schools should innovate both programmatically and in terms of labor agreements, and she indicated at a conference last summer that additional charter-organizing efforts would be under way this year. To house these efforts, she has created a national initiative called the Alliance of Charter Teachers. Most recently, the AFT announced grants to eight teacher unions around the country for what Weingarten calls "entrepreneurial, teacher-driven public education reform." The Chicago

Talent Development High School, the Union Park school, was one of the first grantees.

Officially agnostic on the topic, Secretary of Education Arne Duncan—an ardent supporter of charter schools—is thought by some observers to be enthusiastic about the potential benefits of the unionized charter model.

"The model's perfect for him," says John Ayers, a long-time charter advocate from Chicago who recently became a vice president and treasurer at the Carnegie Foundation for the Advancement of Teaching in California. He notes that the model has a commonsense, middle-ground appeal and challenges both charter operators and teacher unions to move beyond the constant warring of the past.

In speeches, Duncan has singled out Green Dot's efforts to help turn around a massive Los Angeles high school, and he has repeatedly praised teacher unions for taking steps toward innovation and flexibility. In June, Duncan told a conference of charter school advocates, "What distinguishes great charters is not the absence of a labor agreement, but the presence of an educational strategy built around commonsense ideas: more time on task, aligned curricula, high parent involvement, great teacher support, and strong leadership."

Even private foundations have gotten interested in helping charter schools and unions work together. The Eli and Edythe Broad Foundation and The Joyce Foundation recently joined forces to help develop a model charter contract (see "Thin Contracts"). The Bill & Melinda Gates Foundation is funding the AFT Innovation grant program.

Still, efforts to meld charters and unions have had decidedly mixed results.

CHARTERS—AND TEACHERS—GROWING OLDER

In the cases where charter teachers have decided to unionize, the impetus has been to gain more say in how their schools

THIN CONTRACTS

What is a "thin" contract? There's no official definition for these relatively brief contracts that have been negotiated between charter school operators and teachers. The contracts vary widely, but there are some general differences and similarities:

Thin contracts usually apply to a single school site or small network of schools. They require teachers to work a professional workday and don't necessarily include daily start and end times. Salaries can differ based on measures of performance as well as experience and academic qualifications. Employers have to show "just cause" to fire a teacher.

Traditional contracts apply across an entire district. They are generally much longer and more specific. Usually, these contracts detail how much time a teacher has to spend teaching class each day, set a pay scale based on seniority and degrees granted, and provide "due process" protections for teachers against being disciplined or removed from their position. They incorporate state tenure laws.

Both types of contracts include procedures for reporting problems and appealing management decisions. Both are renegotiated at regular intervals and approved by management and teachers.

are run and how they are evaluated, as well as in wages and working conditions. Begun 20 years ago, charter schools are growing older—or at least some of their teachers are.

"A lot of charter schools are doing their work on the backs of teachers willing to work their hearts out," says the University of Chicago's Timothy Knowles, whose Urban Education Institute manages a handful of charter schools. "Class sizes are big, numbers of classes taught are often excessive, basic working conditions are poor, salaries are low, and benefits are worse than those in the traditional public system."

At KIPP: AMP, a school for students from fifth through eighth grades that went through a highly publicized organizing process from 2008–2009, the impact of unionization has been subtle but important. There are fewer and more focused meetings than there were before, according to teacher Kashi Nelson, more regular communication from the principal, and more preparation time. "I love my job again," she says.

Things have also improved for teachers at Chicago's North-town Academy. Citing the new contract, which includes an average salary increase of 10 percent and a new, published salary schedule, Mueller notes, "The teachers are smiling a lot more."

However, some charter school teachers are ambivalent about or even hostile toward teacher unions. Some teachers who supported the union drives at KIPP: AMP and in Chicago changed their minds midway through the process, feeling that the organizing effort was distracting and divisive. Despite the teachers' altered views, their schools were organized, and most teachers remained at the schools. Other than KIPP: AMP, there have been no attempts to unionize at other KIPP New York City schools, according to public affairs director Steve Mancini.

UNIONIZED FROM THE START

While charter school management organizations like KIPP and Civitas have opposed collective bargaining and fought union drives at their schools through legal means, Green Dot schools have been unionized from the start. A longtime Democratic activist whose stepfather was a Teamster, founder Steve Barr feels a strong loyalty to the idea of collective bargaining and insisted on including a union in his model, even though A.J. Duffy, the president of UTLA, wanted nothing to do with negotiating a stripped-down contract at the time (or with Barr, a frequent critic). Barr turned to the California Teachers Association to create a chapter just for Green Dot teachers called Asociación de Maestros Unidos (AMU).

Many of the teachers at Green Dot schools haven't joined the new union, however, though they are still represented (and pay union dues). Last year when the organization took over management of the troubled Locke High School in Watts, teachers found themselves struggling with 800-student "small" schools and crowded classrooms. Frustrated with the lack of timely response from the school, they turned to the protections in the union contract to file a class-size grievance, forcing the school to hire additional teachers, balance teaching loads, and provide added pay for oversized classes and lost preparation periods.

At the end of the year, over 80 percent of teachers at Locke opted to return, compared to 50 percent in previous years. School safety and student retention rates were also up sharply, though academic results stayed flat. "Many of us wouldn't have stayed at Locke if we hadn't been able to get some changes made last year," says art and drama teacher Monica Mayall, the union representative for the school.

The union continues to play a role in the school's second year. "Right now, [school officials] are talking about scheduling teacher observations during prep time, which is against the rules," says Mayall. "But we're going to find a way so that people can volunteer to do it or the faculty can vote on it."

WHO NEEDS WHOM?

Few charter school proponents other than Barr see unionization as playing a significant role in running a successful school. Many involved with charter schools worry that the union presence will eventually infringe on flexibility and the focus on student achievement. "Stories about the length of

Green Dot contracts are instructive," says the University of Chicago's Knowles. "Every time they are renegotiated, they get longer."

While some charter management organizations may position themselves as teacher-friendly and unionize, Knowles predicts that most of them won't see the long-term benefits of unionization. "The majority of the existing charter operators that end up with contracts will get there more like [Civitas] did," he says.

Ayers agrees that charter providers won't be quick to leap at the idea of unionization. He notes that many early charter schools were vehemently anti-union, and some charter school boards are full of business-oriented, anti-union members. "Charter people hate this idea," he says.

"Charter people come up to me all the time and ask 'How do we keep the union out?'" says teachers union watchdog Mike Antonucci, who supports nonunionized charter schools. "That's easy. Keep your employees happy. No happy employee ever said, 'I wish we had a union.'"

Now that states are required to eliminate caps on the number of charters in order to win a share of the $3.4 billion "Race to the Top" fund, charter school advocates may see even less need to reconsider their stance toward unions.

For their part, some union leaders argue that waivers and school-based agreements make it increasingly possible to adapt a school's offerings within the traditional district school system. "A lot of time the media makes it sound like there's no innovation anywhere unless you do drastic things," says Anne Wass, president of the Massachusetts Teachers Association.

One issue on which there is no disagreement is that unionization isn't something that can be jammed down charter teachers' throats. The AFT clearly wants to work with more charter schools, but organizing individual schools is expensive and the union may or may not find many takers.

Back in Chicago, Mueller and the CEO of the charter school organization that runs her school and two others recently signed off on the new 54-page contract. Management challenged the initial organizing effort and forced teachers to repeat the voting process. But it also reversed itself on the six-class workload even before negotiations were begun. Overall retention rates for teachers were higher than in the past.

"Part of it's the economy," says Mueller, who led the negotiations and is running for union president. "But a lot of people want to see how this plays out."

This chapter originally appeared in the January/February 2010 issue of the Harvard Education Letter.

FOR FURTHER INFORMATION

AFT Alliance of Charter School Teachers and Staff: http://www.aftacts.org

Chicago Talent Development High School: http://ctdhs.net/about.htm

S. Dillon. "As Charter Schools Unionize, Many Debate Effect." *New York Times*, July 26, 2009. http://www.nytimes.com/2009/07/27/education/27charter.html

Education Sector. *Growing Pains: Scaling Up the Nation's Best Charter Schools*. Washington, DC: Education Sector, November 24, 2009. Available online at http://www.educationsector.org/research/

National Alliance of Public Charter Schools. *Teacher Leadership in Public Charter Schools*. Washington, DC: National Alliance of Public Charter Schools, October 20, 2008. Available online at http://www.publiccharters.org/publications

NEA page on charter schools: http://www.nea.org/home/16332.htm

PART V

District-Based Improvement

CHAPTER 17

The Real Race to the Top

**To win, your district needs a strategy—
not just a strategic plan**

Rachel E. Curtis and Elizabeth A. City

The Obama administration's planned investments of $100 billion in American Recovery and Reinvestment Act funds and an additional $4 billion in Race to the Top funds offer tremendous opportunities for school systems to focus intently on the work that will bring the greatest learning results for students. However, these new funding programs also have the potential to be just two more things (albeit big things) to which districts react haphazardly. Whether our society will reap a return on these massive investments depends on whether school systems are able to use these funds strategically.

The word *strategy* is most commonly heard in school systems in the context of strategic planning, an exercise districts go through every three to five years or with the arrival of each new superintendent. The sheer number of goals, strategies, and initiatives proposed in most strategic plans actually detracts from the district's ability to focus, and it is often unclear how implementation will lead to improved outcomes for students. As a result, most systems are unable to be precise, agile, and intentional about giving students what they most need to succeed.

That is why it's important for school systems to distinguish between strategy and strategic planning. Stacey Childress of the Harvard Business School defines strategy as "the set of actions an organization chooses to pursue in order to achieve its objectives. These deliberate actions are puzzle pieces that fit together to create a clear picture of how the people, activities, and resources of an organization can work effectively to accomplish a collective purpose." Developing strategy requires systems to identify a few high-leverage ways to improve instruction and student learning. These few, carefully chosen things are well aligned, coherent, mutually reinforcing and add up to a whole that is greater than the sum of its individual parts.

THE POWER OF STRATEGY

Schools and school systems are noisy places. Crises, big and small, come one after another. Local, state, and national politics add to the din. Many systems live in a persistently reactive mode to these external stimuli. We reassure ourselves that we are being responsive (usually a good thing), while in fact we are driven to distraction. The results of all this distraction are predictable—and unacceptable. Improvement efforts are fractured, disconnected, incompletely implemented, and never assessed.

Strategy is about filtering this noise. It's about deciding what systems and the individuals in them must do on behalf of students and their learning, and then putting that decision into action. It provides a focus based on data and beliefs about what will be most effective in helping students learn. By committing to and pursuing strategy, we have a calm center from which to act clearly and deliberately. Crises don't magically disappear, but we approach them with a clearer sense of priority.

Strategic planning is intended to be the vehicle for developing strategy. In high-performing organizations in education and in other sectors, it is. Yet in many school systems, strategic planning reflects a "culture of compliance," in which participants feel they are going through the motions just to satisfy demands imposed from above (only a few of which may be actual federal or state requirements), rather than being empowered to ask probing questions and make informed choices. Planning may also be approached as a community-building activity. Both the compliance and community-building orientations leave systems with plans that tend to be broad, shallow, and not very useful (see "Strategic Plan vs. Strategy").

The reality of how systems improve is dynamic, unlike the neat chart of roles and responsibilities published in a typical

---

STRATEGIC PLAN VS. STRATEGY

A strategic plan typically

- focuses on the status quo
- addresses an external audience
- takes a broad, incremental approach
- includes discrete, unrelated initiatives
- fits within the current structure and culture
- is rarely revised based on new information

A strategy typically

- pursues new ways to accelerate improvement
- addresses an internal audience
- focuses on doing a few things well
- integrates a few key initiatives
- requires people to work together in new ways
- is continually reconsidered and adapted

plan. Without systems in place for discussing implementation, learning from it, and refining the strategy accordingly, the effects of the work are diminished and the plan becomes irrelevant. The answer is not to abandon strategic planning. Instead we must ensure that planning is driven by a clear understanding of strategy and is simply one step in building the system's capacity to act in a focused and coherent way.

THREE QUESTIONS

Schools and school systems that are making substantial progress for children have broken out of a reactive mode and are clear about their answers to three questions: *What* are we doing? *Why* are we doing it? *How* are we doing it? The simplicity of the questions belies the complexity involved in answering them.

What?

Most school systems we know have far too many answers to the question *What are we doing?* Their work is often fragmented, poorly aligned, and limited in its effectiveness. In a system with a robust strategy, there is a clear sense of how the carefully selected initiatives they undertake relate to one another, the organizational changes they require, and the support adults in the system will need.

Why?

Strategic school systems have clear answers to this question. Based on data, research, and discussion, school leaders have bet on a few key initiatives that they believe will have the highest impact on student learning, instead of the myriad other ways their system might invest its resources and energy. And they communicate this rationale to stakeholders throughout the system.

How?

In systems that are improving results for all students, everyone works hard, but more importantly, they work smart. They are strategic in how they approach their work. Leaders in these systems are intentional in word, thought, and action. Amid the constant cacophony of options demanding their attention, they weigh trade-offs, consider evidence, and keep goals in mind. They check assumptions and consider the interrelationship of different improvement efforts. They have an idea of how an action might lead to a particular result, and they adjust their approach based on new information.

FOUR CRITERIA

One way to discern a system's level of strategy is to brainstorm a list of all the initiatives underway in the system, organize them into categories, and assess them on the basis of four criteria: (1) alignment to the instructional core; (2) focus, coherence, and synergy; (3) the degree to which they are *both* visionary *and* problem solving; and (4) ownership and enactment throughout the system (see "Assessing Your System's Level of Strategy").

Instructional Core

Most school systems say they are focused on student learning. Yet a close look at how time and resources are spent in the organization may suggest a very different set of priorities. When a system's strategy is aligned to the instructional core, *all* of its work—including that of the central office and operational departments—is squarely focused on improving student learning and teaching quality.

Focus, Coherence, and Synergy

The elements of an effective strategy should be complementary and mutually reinforcing. For example, a district's strategy

ASSESSING YOUR SYSTEM'S LEVEL OF STRATEGY

A district's senior leadership team can use the following protocol to make sense of the work underway and assess the extent and quality of its system's strategy:

1. Brainstorm all the initiatives underway in the system, write each one on a sticky note, and post them on the wall.

2. Group the sticky notes into categories (e.g., instruction, assessment, curriculum, professional development, technology, operations, and so on). Identify any "orphans"—initiatives that don't fit into any category.

3. Rate the categories from 1 (low) to 4 (high) based on the degree to which they reflect the four criteria for effective strategy (alignment to instructional core; focus, coherence, and synergy; both visionary and problem solving; and ownership and enactment throughout the system).

A system with an effective, coherent strategy will score at least a 3 or 4 on all criteria; the work for the team will be to revisit the strategy to ensure that it is working. A system with mostly 3s and 4s and one score of 1 or 2 has some work to do to ensure the integrity of its strategy. If a system's scores are mostly 1s and 2s, this indicates the need to build a strategy focused on improving student learning.

might focus on improving instruction, developing a student assessment system, and creating a comprehensive student-support system. There are only three big ideas in this strategy. Each supports the others. To take one out of the equation would diminish the effectiveness of the other two.

Both Visionary and Problem Solving

No school system's vision can be attained without fixing serious problems. At the same time, the way problems are solved can help build the capacity needed to realize the vision. For instance, a district whose third-grade literacy scores are low might try to solve the problem by pulling struggling third-grade readers out for interventions to boost their reading levels and scores. This is a backward-looking, reactive approach. Alternatively, they could try to solve that problem in a more visionary way by developing a multipronged structure of support for students, starting in kindergarten, that includes targeted interventions along with efforts to increase how much students read and build their love of reading. This kind of approach addresses the problem in the context of a larger vision of the sorts of readers the system is trying to produce. Such an approach is more forward-looking and proactive.

Ownership and Enactment Throughout the System

The fastest way to know if a system has a strategy is to ask members of the senior leadership team to explain the strategy and give some examples of it in action. The clarity and consistency of response (or lack thereof) is telling. Strategy is enacted when all the people throughout the organization as well as outside partners understand what it is, know what their responsibility for implementing it is, and carry it out.

One of the most striking features of school systems where student achievement results consistently improve is a focus on learning and teaching that pervades all levels of all departments. Everyone is responsible for student learning. No matter how stormy the seas get—budget cuts, reform fads, a thousand other distracting siren songs—these school systems resist being blown off course. Their focus on learning and the data and evidence that measure learning are their "true north," guiding the system with constant reinforcement from senior leadership about what matters most.

Systems in states that win Race to the Top grants may or may not be ready to use that funding strategically. But every state and school system wants to win the *real* race to the top—the one that ensures all students are achieving at high levels, achievement gaps have been closed, and students graduate from high school possessing the knowledge and skills required to choose higher education or meaningful employment that will support them and contribute meaningfully to our democratic society. The fastest runners in that race will be the states and school systems that think and act strategically. In the end, it is the children they serve who will stream across the finish line to win.

This article is adapted from Strategy in Action: How School Systems Can Support Powerful Learning and Teaching, *by Rachel E. Curtis and Elizabeth A. City (Harvard Education Press, 2009), and originally appeared in the November/December 2009 issue of the* Harvard Education Letter.

CHAPTER 18

Creating Coherence in District Administration

A framework based on the work of the Public Education Leadership Project

*Stacey Childress, Richard F. Elmore,
Allen S. Grossman, and Susan Moore Johnson*

Pockets of excellence exist in all school districts. One can find spectacular classes in otherwise dreary schools and stunning schools in mediocre districts. However, to truly serve all students and meet the demands of today's accountability environment, district leaders must find a way for these pockets of excellence to become the norm rather than the exception. This is one of the greatest challenges facing American education today.

What does an urban school district that enables systemwide improvement look like? How is the district organized, and how does it implement a comprehensive strategy to improve student learning? To help leaders of urban school systems answer these questions, 12 faculty members from Harvard Business School and the Harvard Graduate School of Education launched the Public Education Leadership Project (PELP) in 2003. The PELP team set out to identify effective leadership and management practices from both the business and nonprofit sectors that could be adapted to the unique needs of urban districts. The team also spent hundreds of hours observing 15 urban districts of varying sizes across the United States (see "Districts Participating in the Public Education Leadership Project"). Twelve district teams, composed of the superintendent and other leaders, have participated in the PELP programs, discussing a series of leadership and management cases drawn from settings within and outside education.

DISTRICTS PARTICIPATING IN THE PUBLIC EDUCATION LEADERSHIP PROJECT

Aldine, Tex. (56,300 students)
* Anne Arundel County, Md. (74,500)
* Boston, Mass. (57,900)
* Charleston, S.C. (48,500)
* Chicago, Ill. (434,400)
Denver, Colo. (73,000)
Duval County, Fla. (130,000)
* Harrisburg, Pa. (7,900)
Long Beach, Calif. (92,000)
* Memphis, Tenn. (119,000)
* Montgomery County, Md. (146,200)
Philadelphia, Pa. (217,400)
Portland, Ore. (47,000)
* San Diego, Calif. (132,000)
* San Francisco, Calif. (56,200)

* PELP partner districts

For an updated list of PELP partner districts, please visit http://www.hbs.edu/pelp/school.html

Based on its research, the PELP team developed a tool called the PELP Coherence Framework to help district leaders understand and communicate how a school district can be managed to advance and sustain a strategy for achieving high student performance across all schools. *Webster's* defines coherence as "the quality of being logically integrated." In the context of public education, this means that the organizational elements of a school district are synchronized with one another to achieve overarching goals. Often, however, school districts and their practices are more haphazard than purposeful, the product of convenience or history rather than deliberate design.

The PELP Coherence Framework helps leaders recognize the interdependence of multiple parts of their school district—its culture, systems and structures, resources, stakeholder relationships, and environment—and understand how they must reinforce one another to support the successful implementation of a districtwide improvement strategy. PELP participants, now back in their districts, continue to test and refine how best to use the framework in the hard work of building effective organizations.

CREATING A COHERENT ORGANIZATION

At the heart of the PELP Coherence Framework is the *instructional core*, the critical work of teaching and learning that goes on in classrooms. The core includes three interdependent components: a teacher's knowledge and skill, students' engagement in their own learning, and academically challenging content. A district will not see notable improvement in student performance unless there is steady improvement in the instructional core of classes districtwide. Therefore, everything that a district does should support and enable more effective work in the instructional core.

THE PELP COHERENCE FRAMEWORK

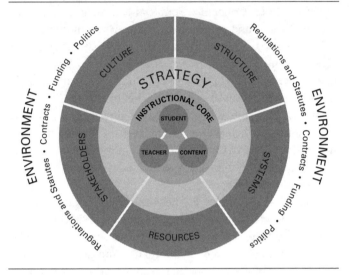

Given the size and complexity of urban school districts, this is an ongoing challenge. To initiate and sustain progress, a district must first have a deliberate, well-articulated *strategy* for improving the instructional core, one that is widely understood and purposefully enacted. Whatever the chosen strategy, the district's subsequent decisions—whether about activities, resources, or organizational structure—should be based on how well each decision will advance the strategy.

The coherence framework is not meant to promote a single or uniform approach for strengthening the instructional core. Districts have demonstrated that effective improvement strategies vary from place to place. For instance, the San Francisco Unified School District pursued an approach designed to capitalize on the strengths of individual schools, allowing principals to choose instructional activities and allocate resources to improve student learning and holding schools accountable for the results. This decentralized approach contrasts with that of the Montgomery County (Md.) Public Schools, where the district office drove the agenda by identifying areas of instructional concern (such as elementary students' reading skills) and provided curricula and professional development programs to support improvement in these areas. Both districts have generated impressive results districtwide and narrowed racial and ethnic achievement gaps.

The PELP program focuses on how a district can gain coherence at the district, school, and classroom levels. The various elements that must work in concert to advance the strategy constitute the remaining parts of the PELP Coherence Framework.

Culture

Culture consists of the prevailing norms and behaviors in an organization—in other words, everyone's shared understanding of "how things work around here." Culture is difficult to change and does not readily respond to edict or slogan. Rather, it must be reshaped gradually by changes in individual practices and beliefs. Successful districts develop a culture where everyone believes that success for all students is attainable.

Despite popular skepticism, over time district leaders can upend an entrenched counterproductive culture and replace it with a dynamic and productive one. They can send important signals about what behaviors they value when they redefine roles or relationships, alter performance expectations, or use job assignments in creative ways. Texas's Aldine Independent School District, for instance, decided on a strategy that focused initially on improving the working relationships among teachers by capitalizing on their knowledge and skills. The district empowered groups of teachers to develop districtwide curricula and work with peers to identify and share effective ways to teach the material. In the process, these educators developed a sense of shared responsibility for the results and a culture of collaboration began to take hold. Efforts in Long Beach (Calif.) Unified School District focused instead on the potential of the principals to lead instructional improvement. School officials convened monthly meetings where principals worked on common challenges. Because the district reassigned each principal to a different school every six years, these school leaders realized that their colleagues' problems could soon become their own. A sense emerged that problems in one school were everyone's responsibility to solve.

Structure

Structure includes how people are organized, who is responsible for results, and who makes or influences decisions. A district's structure may constrain rather than enable high performance and frequently needs to be reworked to support the implementation of an improvement strategy.

Structures can be formal (as shown on an organization chart) or informal (the people you go to when you really need to get something done). Poorly designed formal structures often hinder effective action. In many districts, for instance, a principal does not have direct authority over the people responsible for designing and providing professional development, yet she is held accountable for the results. This arrangement can discourage principals from relying on professional development as a resource for improving instruction.

Informal structures can be even more difficult to manage than formal structures. Power may be based on factors such as proximity, social relationships, or a reputation for getting results. If a strategy is to be implemented effectively, district leaders must understand and influence informal structures. This is especially true if an initiative is controversial or hinges on collaboration. District leaders can use committee assignments and job rotation to reallocate informal power and shape informal structures throughout their districts.

System

School districts are managed through a variety of important systems, such as hiring, career development and promotion, compensation, student assignment, resource allocation, and assessment and accountability. Whether systems are formal or informal, their purpose should be to increase the district's effectiveness in implementing its overall strategy. Effective systems are even-handed and efficient, eliminating the need for individuals to "reinvent the wheel" or "know the right people" to get important things done.

Changes in one system often require adjustments in others. For example, in an effort to attract and hire a cohort of new strong teachers, Boston Public Schools adopted an accelerated timetable, which allowed the district to compete for talent with suburban districts. However, to implement this timetable effectively, principals had to accurately anticipate and report their staffing needs much earlier than in the past and those responsible for recruitment had to develop electronic systems for tracking candidates.

Resources

Money is usually the first thing leaders think about when resources are mentioned, and it is obviously important. But organizational resources also include people, time, facilities, and other assets such as technology and data. District leaders must allocate the full range of resources in ways that are coherent with the district's strategy if the strategy is to be implemented effectively. This means being disciplined about which current and planned activities receive resources and, just as importantly, which ones do not.

San Francisco Unified School District, under the leadership of Superintendent Arlene Ackerman, recognized that funding all schools equally did not ensure that low-performing schools had the resources they needed to improve. In determining a school's basic allocation for 2006–2007, the district employed a weighted student formula that attached a variable dollar amount to every student based on his or her learning needs. A targeted group of underperforming schools received an additional allocation of $431 per student, which the schools used to fund instructional and library materials, parent centers, arts classes, and afterschool programs.

Stakeholder Relationships

Stakeholders are people and groups inside and outside the district that have a legitimate interest in the schools and can influence the success of the district's chosen strategy. These include teachers unions, parents, students, school boards, community and advocacy groups, and local politicians and policymakers. These stakeholders often disagree about what success looks like or how to achieve it. It is especially challenging to get these stakeholders to support a coherent strategy rather than to impose different ones and distract the leaders' focus. District leaders must listen carefully to the diverse views and priorities of those with interests in the schools and draw upon the best of their advice. Ultimately, they must either persuade stakeholder groups about the wisdom of the district's strategy or build an alliance among supporters that is strong enough to prevent others from becoming a disruptive force.

A critical factor in Long Beach's sustained improvement in student performance was the relationship between the staff and the elected board. Carl Cohn, the former superintendent, convened retreats at which the district's staff and board members had to agree unanimously on any major new plans for the district. New plans were then introduced to the community as "board initiatives." Other stakeholders were unable to exploit the typical divisions that exist in many districts between the board and staff.

Environment

A district's environment includes all the external factors that can have an impact on strategy, operations, and performance. The environment in which public school districts operate is especially complex and dynamic, and it includes public and private funding sources, the political and policy context at the city, state, and national levels, and the characteristics of a particular community.

While district leaders have little direct control over their environment, they must nevertheless spend significant time informing and guiding influential parties. Careful investment of time and attention can increase political and financial support for their strategy.

For instance, schools frequently feel pressure to accept grants from private foundations, even when their agendas are not aligned with the district strategy. Thomas Payzant, former superintendent of the Boston Public Schools, would only accept grants from philanthropic sources that supported the district's strategy, which focused on improving instruction and engaging families and communities. He raised almost $100 million during his 10-year tenure, often convincing potential supporters to shift their attention to the district's focus.

The PELP Coherence Framework is designed to focus the attention of public school district leaders on the central problem of increasing the achievement of all students. It helps ensure that the key actions and elements of a district work in concert with one another in support of their strategy. The framework can be useful when evaluating or changing a current strategy, as well as when developing a new one. It provides a common language and consistent way to address the work of achieving organizational coherence. The PELP Coherence Framework has proved to be a useful tool for public education leaders as they strive to create high-performing school districts that are responsive to the increasing external demands for accountability and the enduring needs of students.

This chapter is adapted from Managing School Districts for High Performance: Cases in Public Education Leadership, *edited by Stacey Childress, Richard F. Elmore, Allen S. Grossman, and Susan Moore Johnson (Harvard Education Press, 2007), and originally appeared in the November/December 2007 issue of the* Harvard Education Letter.

About the Contributors

Dara Barlin is associate director of policy for the New Teacher Center.

Kathryn Parker Boudett teaches at the Harvard Graduate School of Education and is the director of the Data Wise Project.

Caroline T. Chauncey is the editor of the *Harvard Education Letter* and assistant director of Harvard Education Publishing Group.

Karin Chenoweth is a long-time education writer who currently writes for The Education Trust.

Stacey Childress is a lecturer at Harvard Business School.

Elizabeth A. City is a lecturer on education and director of the Doctor of Education Leadership Program at the Harvard Graduate School of Education.

Rachel E. Curtis works with school systems, foundations, higher education, and education policy organizations on district improvement strategy and leadership development.

Andreae Downs is a freelance writer living in Massachusetts. She is also a contributing writer to the *Boston Globe*.

Richard F. Elmore is the Gregory R. Anrig Professor of Educational Leadership at the Harvard Graduate School of Education.

Janet Gless is associate director of the New Teacher Center.

Allen S. Grossman is the MBA Class of 1957 Professor of Management Practice at Harvard Business School.

Jan Miles is northwest regional director at the New Teacher Center.

Ellen Moir is founder and executive director of the New Teacher Center.

Susan Moore Johnson is the Jerome T. Murphy Professor at the Harvard Graduate School of Education.

Richard J. Murnane is Juliana W. and William Foss Thompson Professor of Education and Society at the Harvard Graduate School of Education.

W. James Popham is an emeritus professor at the UCLA Graduate School of Education and Information Studies.

Chris Rand is the editorial assistant of the *Harvard Education Letter*.

Robert Rothman is a senior fellow at the Alliance for Excellent Education.

Alexander Russo is an education journalist and spent 2008–2009 as a Spencer Education Fellow at Columbia University's Journalism School.

Jennifer L. Steele is an associate policy researcher at the RAND Corporation.

D. Brent Stephens is the principal of Anthony Ochoa Middle School in Hayward, Calif.

Lee Teitel is a lecturer on education, director of the School Leadership Program, and senior associate for the Executive Leadership Program for Educators at the Harvard Graduate School of Education.

Nancy Walser is the assistant editor of the *Harvard Education Letter*. A former newspaper journalist, Walser served eight years on the Cambridge, Mass., School Committee.